GRILLED CHEESE COOKBOOK

A Bbq and Grilling Cookbook for Your Gathering (Best Grilled Steak Cookbook for Dummies)

Charlotte Delarosa

Published by Sharon Lohan

© **Charlotte Delarosa**

All Rights Reserved

Grilled Cheese Cookbook: A Bbq and Grilling Cookbook for Your Gathering (Best Grilled Steak Cookbook for Dummies)

ISBN 978-1-990334-80-1

All rights reserved. No part of this guide may be reproduced in any form without permission in writing from the publisher except in the case of brief quotations embodied in critical articles or reviews.

Legal & Disclaimer

The information contained in this book is not designed to replace or take the place of any form of medicine or professional medical advice. The information in this book has been provided for educational and entertainment purposes only.

The information contained in this book has been compiled from sources deemed reliable, and it is accurate to the best of the Author's knowledge; however, the Author cannot guarantee its accuracy and validity and cannot be held liable for any errors or omissions. Changes are periodically made to this book. You must consult your doctor or get professional medical advice before using any of the suggested remedies, techniques, or information in this book.

Table of contents

Part 1 1
Grown Up Grilled Cheese 2
Grilled Tomato and Brie 4
Grilled Zucchini Cheese Sandwich 5
Grilled Gruyere with Olive Tapenade 7
Goat Cheese and Honey Fig Sandwiches 9
Turkey Reuben 11
Grilled Cheese with Tomato and Basil Panini and Syrup 12
Mushroom and Manchego Panini 14
Prosciutto and Fig Grilled Cheese 16
Croque-Monsieur 17
Strawberry Grilled Cheese Desserts 18
Spicy Grilled Cheese and Ham 19
Pesto Grilled Cheese Sandwich 20
Baconator Grilled Cheese Sandwich 21
Grilled Apple Cheese Sandwich 22
Jalapeño Popper Grilled Cheese 23
Apple Ham Grilled Cheese 25
Grilled Cheese with a Kick 27
Grilled Cheese and Veggies 28
Broccoli and Ham Grilled Cheese 29
Loaded Grilled Cheese Sandwich 30
Surf and Turf Grilled Cheese 32
College Dorm—Freshman's Sandwich 32
Fire Hot Grilled Cheese 35

Grilled Pork Chops	36
Honey Grilled Pork Chops	37
Lemon Pepper Grilled Pork Chops	37
Tropical Grilled Pork Chops	39
Smoky Grilled Pork Chops	41
Pineapple Grilled Pork Chops	41
Mediterranean Grilled Pork Chops	44
Dijon Grilled Pork Chops	44
Basil Garlic Grilled Pork Chops	45
Bacon and Gouda Stuffed Pork Chops	47
Apple Glazed Pork	48
Grilled Jamaican Jerked Pork Chops	50
Root Beer Pork Chops	52
Grilled Mongolian Pork Chops	54
Grilled Pizza Pork Chops	56
Chesapeake Bay Pork Chops	56
Marinated Pineapple Pork Chops	57
Cherry Chutney Grilled Chops	59
Honey Mustard Grilled Chicken	61
Asian Grilled Chicken	62
Grilled Chicken Adobo	63
Grilled Chicken Teriyaki	63
Grilled Lemon Chicken	65
Rosemary Lemon Grilled Chicken	66
Lime-Tarragon Grilled Chicken	67
Vietnamese Grilled Chicken	67
Cilantro-Lime Grilled Chicken	68

Grilled Five Spice Chicken	70
Lemon Basil Grilled Chicken	72
Grilled Beer Chicken	72
Margarita Grilled Chicken	75
Grilled Hoisin Chicken	76
Grilled Honey-Lemon Chicken	77
BBQ Chicken	78
Cajun Chicken	79
Greek Chicken	80
Grilled Buffalo Wings	81
Grilled Game Hens	81
Thai Grilled Chicken	84
Grilled Sesame Steak	85
Grilled Chipotle Skirt Steak	87
Sirloin Steak with Garlic Butter	88
Jalapeno Steak	89
Barbequed Marinated Flank Steak	90
Beer and Brown Sugar Marinaded Steak	91
Asian Barbequed Steak	92
Korean Marinated Flank Steak	93
Whiskey Marinated Steak	94
Port Wine Marinaded Flank Steak	95
Mango Spiced Steak Skewers	96
Margarita Grilled Shrimp	98
Honey Grilled Shrimp	99
Spicy Grilled Shrimp	99
Grilled Shrimp Scampi	101

Spicy Coconut and Lime Grilled Shrimp 102

Sweet and Spicy Grilled Shrimp 102

Grilled Garlic and Herb Shrimp 104

Basil Shrimp 106

Thai Spiced Barbecue Shrimp 106

Chipotle Grilled Shrimp 108

Spicy Lime Grilled Shrimp 109

Cajun Grilled Veggies 109

Smoky Grilled Vegetables 111

Herb Grilled Vegetables 112

Grilled Zucchini Slices 113

Balsamic Grilled Zucchini 114

Grilled Garlic Parmesan Zucchini 115

Grilled Italian Dressing Asparagus 116

Grilled Soy-Sesame Asparagus 117

Grilled Eggplant 118

Grilled Cabbage 119

Coconut and Lime Grilled Kale 120

Grilled Fava Beans 120

Grilled Cauliflower 121

Grilled Potatoes 123

Grilled Caramelized Onions 124

Grilled Sweet Potatoes with Apples 125

Grilled Portobello Mushrooms with Blue Cheese 126

Pesto Stuffed Grilled Portobellos 127

Part 2 128

Introduction 129

1: Grilled Chicken with Pineapple 131
2: Stuffed Grilled Bell Peppers 133
4: Philly Grilled Cheesesteak Sandwich 135
5: Grilled Jalapeno Poppers Wrapped in Bacon 137
6: Grilled Dijon and Maple Chicken 139
7: Grilled Honey Cilantro and Lime Chicken 141
8: Grilled Barbecue Chicken Hawaiian Style 143
9: Grilled Kansas City Pork Chops 145
10: Grilled Ranch and Bacon Potatoes 147
11: Grilled Garlic Steak Skewers Asian Style 149
12: Grilled Sweet Potatoes 151
13: Grilled Rum and Coconut Shrimp 153
14: Grilled Harissa Moroccan Chicken 155
15: Grilled Shrimp Melody 157
16: Honey Mustard Grilled Pork 159
17: Grilled Chicken with Herbs and Lemon 161
18: Grilled Garlic Bread 163
19: Grilled Chicken Key West Style 165
20: Grilled Asada Carne 167
21: Grilled Pineapple Sriracha Chicken 169
22: Grilled Brown Sugar Steak in Whisky 171
23: Grilled Teriyaki Turkey Burgers with Onions and Pineapples 173
24: Grilled Chicken with Lemon 176
25: Grilled Soy and Honey Pork Chops 178
26: Grilled Crostini with Avocado Caprese 180
27: Grilled Shrimp with Pineapple and Coconut 182

28: Grilled Barbeque Ribs 184
29: Grilled Eggplant 186
30: Grilled Zucchini 188
Conclusion 189

Part 1

Grown Up Grilled Cheese

Serves: 4
Cooking Time: 15 minutes

Ingredients

1 cup red onion, sliced
1 T minced garlic
1 cup Cheddar cheese, white, shredded
8 slices bread
2 cups spinach
tomato slices
½ lb bacon, cooked

Directions

1. Most of these grilled cheese sandwiches will have the standard assemble and cooking instructions, So when you see *Standard assembly and grill you can follow the breakdown here in recipe One

I. Use nonstick spray or butter and heat a skillet.
II. Add the bread over the cheese followed by the fillings (in this case it is ½ cup spinach, onion blend and a few slices of bacon).
III. Add the top slice of bread to the sandwich and grill both sides of bread for 1 to 2 minutes each.
IV. Serve when the cheese has melted.

Nutritional Information

Calories 376, Fat 11g, Carbohydrates 50.3g, Protein 20.2g

Grilled Tomato and Brie

Serves: 4
Cooking Time: 15 minutes

Ingredients

8 slices bread, whole grain (or your choice)
1 tsp olive oil
1 T garlic, minced
2 tsp sweet honey Dijon spread
4 oz Brie cheese, sliced
1 1/3 cups baby arugula and spinach
6 slices tomatoes, beefsteak, sliced

Directions

I. Assemble the sandwich by spreading the Dijon on the slices of bread.
II. Spray the grill rack or add butter to the outer slices of bread.
III. Add the assembled sandwiches to the grill.
IV. Grill bread on each side for about 1 to 2 minutes.

Nutritional Information

Calories 234, Fat 10.1g, Carbohydrates 26.9g, Protein 11g

Grilled Zucchini Cheese Sandwich

Serves: 4
Cooking Time: 15 minutes

Ingredients

1 zucchini, sliced
4 tsp EVOO
1 T minced garlic
1 1/2 tsp balsamic vinegar
1/8 tsp salt and pepper to taste
4 ciabatta rolls (bread)
lettuce, large leaves or basil leaves
Mozzarella cheese, sliced

Directions

I. Sauté the zucchini in a skillet with a little bit of oil and garlic. Toss and cook for about 2 to 3 minutes.
II. Drizzle oil over the zucchini and sprinkle with salt and pepper to taste.
III. Brush the bottoms of the bread (ciabatta rolls) with the oil and assemble the grilled cheese sandwiches.
IV. Wrap the assembled sandwiches in foil and heat in the oven for about 5 to 7 minutes or microwave for 10 to 15 seconds.

Nutritional Information

Calories 343, Fat 16.8g, Carbohydrates 35.3g, Protein 15.4g

Grilled Gruyere with Olive Tapenade

Serves: 4
Cooking Time: 15 to 20 minutes

Ingredients

1 jar sun-dried tomatoes
12 pitted olives
2 garlic cloves, minced
8 slices bread
8 tomatoes, thickly sliced
2 to 3 oz Gruyère cheese, shaved

Directions

I. Combine the tomatoes and first three ingredients into a blender or food processor and blend until smooth.
II. Brush the bread with a little extra oil on one side of each sandwich and spread the mix on the other side.
III. Divide the remaining ingredients up for four sandwiches and assemble the sandwiches with the remaining ingredients.
IV. Use nonstick spray or butter and heat a skillet.
V. Add the bread over the cheese.
VI. Add the top slice of bread to the sandwich and grill both sides of bread for 1 to 2 minutes each.
VII. Serve when the cheese has melted.

Nutritional Information

Calories 346, Fat 20.2g, Carbohydrates 28.9g, Protein 14.7g

Goat Cheese and Honey Fig Sandwiches

Serves: 4
Cooking Time: 15 to 20 minutes

Ingredients

2 tsp honey
¼ tsp lemon
1 package Goat cheese
8 slices cinnamon raisin bread
2 T fig jelly
2 tsp basil, fresh, thinly sliced
sugar, powdered to taste

Directions

I. Blend the first three ingredients in a small bowl until well combined and smooth.
II. Start assembling the sandwich with the Goat cheese first, then preserves spread over the inside of the other slice of bread.
III. Add the remaining ingredients and bread.
IV. Spread butter on the outside of both slices of bread for each sandwich.
V. Use nonstick spray or butter and heat a skillet.
VI. Grill both sides of the bread for 1 to 2 minutes each.

Nutritional Information

Calories 243, Fat 8.5g, Carbohydrates 33.1g, Protein 9.8g

Turkey Reuben

Serves: 4
Cooking Time: 15 minutes

Ingredients

2 T mustard, Dijon
8 slices bread, rye
4 slices Swiss cheese
8 oz turkey, smoked, sliced
2/3 cup sauerkraut, rinsed
1/4 cup Thousand Island dressing
1 T canola oil

Directions

I. Spread the Dijon mustard on each slice of bread and assemble the grilled turkey and cheese sandwiches.
II. Use nonstick spray or butter and heat a skillet.
III. Grill both sides of the bread for 1 to 2 minutes each.
IV. Serve warm with a dill pickle or chips on the side.

Nutritional Information

Calories 255, Fat 10.7g, Carbohydrates 18.9g, Protein 19.6g

Grilled Cheese with Tomato and Basil Panini and Syrup

Serves: 4
Cooking Time: 20 minutes

Ingredients

½ cup balsamic vinegar
1 slice Cuban bread
1 T EVOO
basil leaves, large
5 oz Mozzarella cheese
2 tomatoes, sliced
¼ tsp salt and pepper to taste

Directions

I. Boil the vinegar and reduce down to 3 T, which could take about 6 to 7 minutes.
II. Brush the oil over the bread on one side and assemble the sandwiches.
III. Use nonstick spray or butter and heat a skillet.
IV. Grill both sides of the bread for 1 to 2 minutes each.

Nutritional Information

Calories 325, Fat 13.4g, Carbohydrates 37.4g, Protein 13.6g

Mushroom and Manchego Panini

Serves: 4
Cooking Time: 15 to 20 minutes

Ingredients

1 tsp butter, unsalted
¼ cup shallots, minced
1 T thyme, chopped
½ tsp salt and pepper to taste
2 cans blended mushrooms, sliced
1 can cremini mushrooms
1 ½ T sherry vinegar
8 slices sourdough bread
3 oz Manchego cheese, shaved
1 garlic clove, minced

Directions

I. Sauté the vegetables and cook for about 5 to 7 minutes.
II. Divide the cooked vegetables between the 4 sandwiches.
III. Assemble the rest of the sandwich.
IV. Spray the skillet and grill for 2 to 3 minutes on each side until the cheese has melted.

Nutritional Information

Calories 352, Fat 10.9g, Carbohydrates 48.8g, Protein 16.8g

Prosciutto and Fig Grilled Cheese

Serves: 4
Cooking Time: 15 to 20 minutes

Ingredients

8 slices Italian bread
4 oz sliced prosciutto, sliced
1 ¼ cup Fontana, shredded
½ cup spinach, baby
¼ cup fig preserves
olive oil

Directions

I. Grill the Italian bread first.
II. Assemble the sandwiches after you have grilled the bread.
III. Add the sandwiches to a heated skillet with just a little oil until the cheese has melted.

Nutritional Information

Calories 345, Fat 13g, Carbohydrates 37.1g, Protein 18.2g

START – review backwards

Croque-Monsieur

Serves: 4
Cooking Time: 15 to 20 minutes

Ingredients

4 slices French bread
4 tsp honey mustard
6 oz deli ham, sliced
4 slices Swiss cheese
½ cup skim milk
3 large egg whites

Directions

I. Form pockets in the bread by cutting slits and spread the honey mustard into each pocket.
II. Add the ham and cheese into each pocket.
III. Whisk egg and milk in a bowl and dip the sandwiches in the bowl.
IV. Heat a skillet and grill each sandwich one at a time. Make sure it is grilled and cooked on each end.

Nutritional Information

Calories 293, Fat 9.8g, Carbohydrates 27.9g, Protein 22.3g

Strawberry Grilled Cheese Desserts

Serves: 2
Cooking Time: 10 to 15 minutes

Ingredients

strawberry preserves
balsamic vinegar
Brioche cheese
Mascarpone cheese
butter

Directions

I. Spread the butter over the bread.
II. Assemble the sandwiches.
III. Use nonstick spray or butter and heat a skillet.
IV. Grill both sides of the bread for 1 to 2 minutes each.
V. Serve warm.

Nutritional Information

Calories 348, Fat 16.3g, Carbohydrates 27.2g, Protein 23.4g

Spicy Grilled Cheese and Ham

Serves: 1
Cooking Time: 10 to 15 minutes

Ingredients

2 slices Swiss cheese
2 slices deli ham
2 green chile peppers
2 slices bread, rye
1 T butter

Directions

I. Assemble the sandwich and butter both sides of the bread.
II. Heat the grill or skillet, and cook on both sides until the bread is toasted and the cheese has melted inside the sandwich.

Nutritional Information

Calories 312, Fat 13.7g, Carbohydrates 28.9g, Protein 14.4g

Pesto Grilled Cheese Sandwich

Serves: 1
Cooking Time: 10 minutes

Ingredients

2 slices bread, Italian or sourdough
1 T butter
1 T pesto sauce
1 slice Provolone cheese
2 slices tomato, thin
1 slice American cheese

Directions

I. Spread butter over the outside of the slices of bread and also spread the pesto sauce on one or both slices on the inside of the bread.
II. Once you have spread the pesto sauce on the inside of the sandwich, assemble the rest of the sandwich.
III. Use nonstick spray or butter and heat a skillet.
IV. Grill both sides of the bread for 1 to 2 minutes each.

Nutritional Information

Calories 609, Fat 19.6g, Carbohydrates 64.4g, Protein 47.6g

Baconator Grilled Cheese Sandwich

Serves: 4
Cooking Time: 15 minutes

Ingredients

8 slices bacon, cooked
¼ C butter
8 slices bread (your choice)
sliced American cheese
8 slices tomato

Directions

I. Cook the bacon to desired tenderness.
II. Spread butter on the outer side of each slice of bread.
III. Assemble 4 sandwiches.
IV. Use nonstick spray or butter and heat a skillet.
V. Grill both sides of the bread for 2 to 3 minutes each or until cheese has melted.

Nutritional Information

Calories 406, Fat 31g, Carbohydrates 17.4g, Protein 15.7g

Grilled Apple Cheese Sandwich

Serves: 1
Cooking Time: 10 to 15 minutes

Ingredients

2 slices bread
1 1/2 tsp olive oil
1/2 apple, granny smith, peeled and thinly sliced
1/3 cup Swiss cheese, shredded

Directions

I. Brush oil over one side of each slice of bread.
II. Lay the bread in a skillet with the oil side down.
III. Arrange the apples over the top followed by the cheese.
IV. Add the other slice of bread with the oil side out.
V. Cook for 2 to 3 minutes on each side until the cheese melts and the bread has browned to a golden color.

Nutritional Information

Calories 316, Fat 15.8g, Carbohydrates 18g, Protein 10.3g

Jalapeño Popper Grilled Cheese

Serves: 2
Cooking Time: 10 to 15 minutes

Ingredients

2 oz cream cheese
1 T sour cream
10 to 12 pickled jalapeño peppers, chopped
ciabatta rolls
4 tsp butter
8 tortillas, crushed
½ cup blended cheese, shredded

Directions

I. Combine the cream cheese, jalapeños and sour cream in a bowl, set aside.
II. Slice the rolls in half and cut again so that they have a flat top.
III. Spread butter over the outside of the bread.
IV. Assemble the sandwiches by spreading the jalapeño blend over the insides of the buns. Include the tortillas that have been torn into pieces.
V. Grill over medium heat in the preheated skillet until cheese is runny and melted to the bread.

Nutritional Information

Calories 276, Fat 18.9g, Carbohydrates 19.9g, Protein 7.5g

Apple Ham Grilled Cheese

Serves: 2
Cooking Time: 10 minutes

Ingredients

4 slices ham
1 apple, peeled, cored
1 T mayo
2 slices cheddar
4 slices bread
2 T butter
2 eggs
4 T milk

Directions

I. Combine the ham and apple and spread this out onto two different slices of bread.
II. Assemble the sandwiches and add butter to the outside slices.
III. Whisk the eggs and milk in a bowl, dip the sandwiches into the bowl.
IV. Fry the sandwiches in a skillet for about 2 to 3 minutes on each side until they are crispy and the cheese is melted.

Nutritional Information

Calories 598, Fat 48.7g, Carbohydrates 41.8g, Protein 14.7g

Grilled Cheese with a Kick

Serves: 2
Cooking Time: 10 minutes

Ingredients

¼ cup mango chutney
4 slices bread, stale, crusty or toasted
6 slices deli ham, black forest
4 slices Cheddar cheese, white
2 T butter

Directions

I. Spread the chutney over the bread, then add ham and then the cheese.
II. Butter the outsides of the bread.
III. Use nonstick spray or butter and heat a skillet.
IV. Grill both sides of the bread for 1 to 2 minutes each or until the cheese is melted.

Nutritional Information

Calories 420, Fat 21.7g, Carbohydrates 35g, Protein 23.8g

Grilled Cheese and Veggies

Serves: 4
Cooking Time: 10 to 15 minutes

Ingredients

1 ½ cup coleslaw mix
½ cup bean sprouts
8 slices bread, sourdough
3 T butter
3 T honey mustard
6 oz Havarti cheese, sliced

Directions

I. Toss the slaw mix with the bean sprouts
II. Add butter to one side of each of the 8 slices of bread and spread honey mustard on the opposite sides of the bread.
III. Assemble the sandwiches with the slaw and bean mixture and then the cheese.
IV. Close the sandwiches and grill in an open skillet for 2 to 3 minutes on each side or until the cheese is melted.

Nutritional Information

Calories 228, Fat 3.6g, Carbohydrates 27.4g, Protein 24.4g

Broccoli and Ham Grilled Cheese

Serves: 1
Cooking Time: 10 to 15 minutes

Ingredients

2 slices bread, whole grain
1/4 Sharp Cheddar cheese
1/4 cup Parmesan cheese, grated
1/4 cup ham, cooked
1 lb broccoli florets, steamed, diced
1/8 tsp garlic powder
salt and pepper to taste
1 T olive oil

Directions

I. Combine everything but the ham in a bowl.
II. Layer everything over one slice of bread, spread out.
III. Spread butter over the outer pieces and grill for 2 to 3 minutes on each side.

Nutritional Information

Calories 169, Fat 9.2g, Carbohydrates 13.8g, Protein 8.4g

Loaded Grilled Cheese Sandwich

Serves: 2
Cooking Time: 1 hour

Ingredients

1 T butter
1 T vegetable oil
2 red onions, sliced
1 garlic clove, minced
½ cup sugar
½ tsp salt and pepper to taste
½ cup red wine vinegar
½ cup fruit red wine, dry

Sandwich

4 slices bread, sourdough or rye
2 T butter
4 slices pastrami
4 oz Swiss cheese, shredded
2 T mustard, whole grain

Directions

I. Melt the butter in a skillet and sauté the garlic, onion and seasonings.

II. You want to be sure to stir everything well until it is well combined.
III. Lower the heat to a steady simmer and cook until the onions are soft and brown. This could take approximately 15 to 20 minutes.
IV. Add in the vinegar and wines, stirring every few minutes. Everything should thicken, then remove from the heat. It will continue to thicken as it cools.
V. Start to assemble the sandwiches as you would a traditional grilled cheese. But when you spread butter on the outside of the bread, the inside will have marmalade spread over them. Add meat and cheese to the sandwiches and then mustard over the top of the sandwich fillings.
VI. Grill or cook in the skillet until the cheese is melted and the bread is a light golden-brown color.

Nutritional Information

Calories 660, Fat 34g, Carbohydrates 51g, Protein 33g

Surf and Turf Grilled Cheese

Serves: 2
Cooking Time: 20 minutes

Ingredients

4 slices bread, sourdough
2 T mayo
pepper, white
2 T butter
½ lb crab, cooked, canned
½ avocado, sliced
2 red onions, sliced
4 oz Swiss cheese or other preferred cheese

Directions

I. Spread mayo over one side of the slices of bread.
II. On the opposite side, spread butter.
III. Sprinkle white pepper and layer the fillings over the mayo and assemble the sandwiches.
IV. Cook or grill in a preheated skillet until the bread is toasted and the cheese is melted.

Nutritional Information

Calories 757, Fat 47g, Carbohydrates 38g, Protein 46g

College Dorm—Freshman's Sandwich

Serves: 1
Cooking Time: 25 minutes

Ingredients

1 T butter
2 T cream cheese, soft is best
2 slices bread, sourdough or rye
1 slice Fontina cheese
1 slice Cheddar cheese
¼ cup artichokes, canned, dried
black olives to taste
2 slices tomatoes, thick

Directions

I. Spread butter over the outside of both slices of bread.
II. On the inside, spread the cream cheese over one slice.
III. Assemble the sandwich with the remaining ingredients and season to taste with the salt and pepper.
IV. Heat the skillet or griddle and cook/grill until the cheese is melted and the bread is toasted to desired crispness.

Nutritional Information

Calories 631, Fat 43g, Carbohydrates 40g, Protein 23g

Fire Hot Grilled Cheese

Serves: 1
Cooking Time: 15 minutes

Ingredients

2 slices bread, sourdough
2 jalapeño peppers, seeded and thinly sliced
1 slice tomato
2 slices pepper jack
1 slice American cheese
2 dabs hot sauce
habanero peppers, thinly sliced

Directions

I. Assemble the sandwich with all the peppers and cheese.
II. Spread butter on the outside of each slice.
III. Use nonstick spray or butter and heat a skillet.
IV. Grill both sides of the bread for 1 to 2 minutes each or until the cheese is melted.
V. This is a hot sandwich (consider yourself warned).

Nutritional Information

Calories 547, Fat 38.2g, Carbohydrates 47g, Protein 21.3g

Grilled Pork Chops

Honey Grilled Pork Chops

Ingredients:
- 4 1" thick boneless pork chops
- 1/4 cup honey
- 2 tblsp. Dijon mustard
- 1 tblsp. orange juice
- 1/4 tsp. dried tarragon
- 1 tsp. cider vinegar
- 1/2 tsp. Worcester sauce
- 1/8 tsp. garlic powder

Directions:
1. Preheat grill.
2. Brush rack with vegetable oil.
3. Trim excess fat from chops.
4. Score outer edge of meat at 1" intervals.
5. Blend honey, mustard, orange juice, tarragon, vinegar, Worcestershire sauce and garlic powder in a small bowl.
6. Place chops on the grill about 4 inches from heat.
7. Brush with honey mixture.
8. Grill for 8 minutes, brushing every 2 minutes with honey mixture.
9. Turn chops over.
10. Grill for 8 minutes longer or until cooked through, basting every 2 minutes with honey mixture.
11. Serve and enjoy!

Lemon Pepper Grilled Pork Chops

Ingredients:

1/2 cup water
1/3 cup light soy sauce
1/4 cup vegetable oil
3 tbsps. lemon pepper seasoning
2 tsps. minced garlic
6 boneless pork loin chops, trimmed of fat
   Directions:
1. Mix water, soy sauce, vegetable oil, lemon pepper seasoning, and minced garlic in a deep bowl; add pork chops and marinate in refrigerator at least 2 hours.
2. Preheat an outdoor grill for medium-high heat and lightly oil the grate.
3. Remove pork chops from the marinade and shake off excess. Discard the remaining marinade.
4. Cook the pork chops on the preheated grill until no longer pink in the center, 5 to 6 minutes per side. An instant-read thermometer inserted into the center should read 145 degrees F (63 degrees C).

Tropical Grilled Pork Chops

Ingredients:

1 clove garlic, minced
1 tsp. chili powder
1/4 tsp. cayenne pepper
1 pod cardamom seeds
1/2 tsp. water, or as needed
1 tsp. vegetable oil
1/4 cup rice wine vinegar
1/2 cup sugar
1 mango - peeled, seeded, and chopped
1/4 tsp. salt
1/2 tsp. cilantro
2 tsps. lemon juice
1 fresh jalapeno pepper, minced
1 1/2 cups unsweetened applesauce
3 pineapple rings, chopped
1 pinch white pepper
1/3 cup soy sauce
1/3 cup rice wine vinegar
6 pork chops

Directions:

1. With a mortar and pestle, mash together the garlic, chili powder, cayenne, and cardamom seeds.
2. Mix in enough water to form a paste.
3. Heat the oil in a saucepan over medium heat.
4. Stir in spice paste, and cook until it begins to bubble, about 30 seconds.
5. Stir in vinegar; cook without boiling for 2 minutes.
6. Stir in sugar until it dissolves.

7. Mix in mango, salt, cilantro, lemon juice, and jalapeno; simmer 20 minutes.
8. Stir in applesauce and pineapple; simmer 10 minutes more.
9. Season with white pepper.
10. Place in a bowl, cover, and refrigerate until ready to use.
11. To prepare marinade, mix 2/3 cup of the salsa with soy sauce and 1/3 cup vinegar.
12. Place pork chops in a large resealable plastic bag, and pour marinade over chops. Seal tightly, and place in the refrigerator for 1 hour.
13. Prepare grill for medium-high heat.
14. Drain marinade from bag, and heat in a saucepan until boiling.
15. Lightly oil grill grate.
16. Place pork chops on the hot grill.
17. Cook 10 minutes, or to desired doneness, turning once and basting occasionally with the boiled marinade.
18. Warm remaining salsa over medium-low heat. Serve pork chops topped with the salsa.

Smoky Grilled Pork Chops

Ingredients:
- 1 tbsp. seasoned salt
- 1 tsp. ground black pepper
- 1 tbsp. garlic powder
- 1 tbsp. onion powder
- 1 tbsp. ground paprika
- 2 tsps. Worcestershire sauce
- 1 tsp. liquid smoke flavoring
- 4 bone-in pork chops (1/2 to 3/4 inch thick)

Directions:
1. Preheat an outdoor grill for medium heat, and lightly oil the grate.
2. In a bowl, mix together the seasoned salt, black pepper, garlic powder, onion powder, paprika, Worcestershire sauce, and smoke flavoring until thoroughly combined.
3. Rinse pork chops, and sprinkle the wet chops on both sides with the spice mixture. With your hands, massage the spice rub into the meat; allow to stand for 10 minutes.
4. Grill the chops over indirect heat until no longer pink inside, about 12 minutes per side. An instant-read thermometer should read at least 145 degrees F (63 degrees C).
5. Allow chops to stand for 10 more minutes before serving.

Pineapple Grilled Pork Chops

Ingredients:

1 (8 oz.) can pineapple rings, juice drained and reserved
1/4 cup brown sugar
1/4 cup soy sauce
1/4 tsp. garlic powder
4 pork chops
1 pinch ground black pepper

Directions:
1. Mix together the drained pineapple juice, brown sugar, soy sauce, and garlic powder together in a large plastic zipper bag, and smush the bag a few times with your hands to mix the marinade and dissolve the sugar.
2. Place the pork chops into the marinade, squeeze out any air in the bag, seal it, and refrigerate overnight.
3. Reserve the pineapple rings.
4. Preheat an outdoor grill for medium heat, and lightly oil the grate.
5. Remove the chops from the marinade, shaking off excess, and grill until browned, the meat is no longer pink inside, and the meat shows good grill marks, 5 to 8 minutes per side.
6. Brush several times with marinade and let the marinade cook onto the surface of the meat.
7. Discard excess marinade.
8. While the meat is grilling, place 4 pineapple rings onto the grill, and allow to cook until hot and the slices show grill marks; serve the chops topped with the grilled pineapple rings.

Mediterranean Grilled Pork Chops

Ingredients:
2 tsps. dried sage, crumbled
2 tsps. dried rosemary leaves, crumbled
1 tsp. dried thyme
1 tsp. fennel seed, crushed
1/2 tsp. white sugar
1 bay leaf, crumbled1
1/2 tsps. salt
4 bone-in pork rib chops (not pork loin chops)
1/3 cup extra-virgin olive oil

Directions:
1. In a bowl, mix together the sage, rosemary, thyme, fennel seed, sugar, bay leaf, and salt until thoroughly combined.
2. Rub both sides of the pork chops with the herb mixture, and coat them with olive oil. Refrigerate several hours or overnight.
3. Preheat an outdoor grill for medium heat, and lightly oil the grate.
4. Grill the chops until they are browned, show good grill marks, and the meat is no longer pink inside, about 4 minutes per side. An instant-read meat thermometer inserted into the thickest part of a chop should read at least 145 degrees F (63 degrees C).

Dijon Grilled Pork Chops

Ingredients:
6 tbsps. Dijon mustard

6 tbsps. brown sugar
3 tbsps. unsweetened apple juice
3 tbsps. Worcestershire sauce
4 (8 oz.) bone-in pork loin chops

Directions:
1. Mix mustard, brown sugar, apple juice, and Worcestershire sauce together in a bowl until marinade is smooth.
2. Pour 2/3 the marinade into a large resealable plastic bag.
3. Add pork chops, coat with marinade, squeeze out excess air, and seal the bag. Marinate in the refrigerator for 8 hours to overnight.
4. Cover bowl with remaining marinade with plastic wrap and refrigerate.
5. Remove pork chops from marinade and discard bag and marinade.
6. Preheat grill for medium heat and lightly oil the grate.
7. Cook the pork chops on the preheated grill, basting with reserved marinade, until no longer pink in the center, 4 to 5 minutes per side. An instant-read thermometer inserted into the center should read 145 degrees F (63 degrees C).
8. Let pork chops stand for 5 minutes before serving.

Basil Garlic Grilled Pork Chops

Ingredients:
4 (8 oz.) pork chops
1 lime, juiced

4 cloves garlic, minced
1/4 cup chopped fresh basil
Salt and black pepper to taste

Directions:
1. Toss the pork chops with the lime juice in a bowl until evenly covered.
2. Toss with garlic and basil.
3. Season the chops to taste with salt and pepper. Set aside to marinate for 30 minutes.
4. Preheat an outdoor grill for medium heat, and lightly oil the grate.
5. Cook the pork chops on the preheated grill until no longer pink in the center, 5 to 10 minutes per side.
6. An instant-read thermometer inserted into the center should read 145 degrees F (63 degrees C).

Bacon and Gouda Stuffed Pork Chops

Ingredients:

2 oz. smoked Gouda cheese, shredded
4 slices bacon, cooked and crumbled
1/4 cup chopped fresh parsley
1/8 tsp. ground black pepper
2 (2 1/4 inch thick) center-cut, bone-in pork chops
1 tsp. olive oil
1/4 tsp. salt
Ground black pepper

Directions:

1. Preheat an outdoor grill for medium heat.
2. In a small bowl, combine the cheese, bacon, parsley, and 1/8 tsp. black pepper.
3. Lay the chop flat on cutting board, and with a sharp knife held parallel to the board, cut a pocket into the pork, going all the way to the bone, but leaving the sides intact.
4. Stuff cheese mixture into pocket, and close with a wooden toothpick. Brush meat with oil, and season with salt and more black pepper.
5. Lightly oil the grill grate.
6. Grill over medium heat for 5 to 8 minutes on each side, or until pork is done. Careful not to overcook!

Apple Glazed Pork

Ingredients:
4 Granny Smith apples, cored and chopped
1 (8 oz.) can crushed pineapple, with juice
1/2 cup apple cider vinegar
1/4 cup brown sugar
1/4 cup Dijon mustard
1/4 cup water
2 tbsps. honey
4 cloves garlic, crushed
2 tsps. cayenne pepper
1 tsp. onion powder
6 boneless pork chops

Directions:
1. Place apples, pineapple and juice, vinegar, sugar, mustard, water, honey, garlic, cayenne pepper, and onion powder in a large saucepan.
2. Bring to a boil over high heat, then reduce heat to medium-low, cover, and simmer until the apples are tender, about 15 minutes. Allow the mixture to cool to room temperature, then puree in a blender until smooth.
3. Place the pork chops into a resealable plastic bag, and pour the apple puree overtop. Marinate in the refrigerator overnight.
4. Preheat an outdoor grill for medium heat, and lightly oil grate.
5. Remove pork chops from marinade, and shake off excess. Discard remaining marinade.

6. Cook on preheated grill until the chops are no longer pink in the center, about 5 minutes per side depending on the thickness.

Grilled Jamaican Jerked Pork Chops

Ingredients:

1/2 (12 oz.) bottle lager style beer
3 fluid oz. dark rum
1/4 cup molasses
1/4 cup soy sauce
1/4 cup lime juice
2 tbsps. minced garlic
2 tbsps. minced ginger
1 scotch bonnet chile pepper, minced
2 tsps. chopped fresh thyme
2 tsps. chopped fresh marjoram
1 1/2 tsps. ground allspice
2 tsps. ground cinnamon
1 tsp. ground nutmeg
2 bay leaves
8 (6 oz.) pork loin chops
Kosher salt and cracked black pepper to taste

Directions:

1. Pour the beer, rum, molasses, soy sauce, and lime juice into a bowl.
2. Stir in the garlic, ginger, scotch bonnet pepper, thyme, and marjoram.
3. Season with allspice, cinnamon, nutmeg, and bay leaves.
4. Place the pork chops into a zip top bag, and pour in the marinade. Refrigerate overnight.
5. Prepare an outdoor grill for medium heat.

6. Take the pork chops out of the marinade, place on a plate, and allow to sit at room temperature for 15 to 20 minutes as the grill heats.
7. Season the chops to taste with kosher salt and cracked black pepper.
8. Grill the chops on both sides until a thermometer inserted into the center registers 145 degrees F (63 degrees C).
9. Allow the pork chops to rest for about 5 minutes before serving to allow the juices to redistribute.

Root Beer Pork Chops

Ingredients:

4 (1-inch thick) pork chops
3 (12 fluid oz.) cans or bottles root beer
Salt and pepper to taste
1 cup beef stock
2 tbsps. brown sugar
1/2 tsp. chipotle-flavored hot sauce
2 tsps. Worcestershire sauce
1 pinch salt, to taste

Directions:

1. Place the pork chops in a dish; pour 2 cans of the root beer over the chops.
2. Place in refrigerator to marinate at least 2 hours.
3. Remove the pork chops from the root beer; season with salt and pepper.
4. Combine the remaining can of root beer, the beef stock, brown sugar, hot sauce, and Worcestershire sauce in a saucepan over medium heat; simmer the mixture until it reduces to about 3/4 cup. Set aside.
5. Preheat an outdoor grill for medium-high heat, and lightly oil the grate.
6. Grill the pork chops on the preheated grill until the no longer pink in the center, about 8 minutes per side.
7. An instant-read thermometer inserted into the center should read 145 degrees F (63 degrees C).
8. Brush the chops generously with the reduction sauce and continue cooking for about 2 minutes more per side.

9. Remove from grill and brush with any remaining sauce.
10. Season with salt to taste before serving.

Grilled Mongolian Pork Chops

Ingredients:
1/2 cup hoisin sauce
4 cloves garlic, minced1
1/2 tbsps. soy sauce
1 tbsp. grated fresh ginger
1 tbsp. red wine vinegar
1 tbsp. rice vinegar
1 tbsp. sherry vinegar
2 tsps. sesame oil
2 tsps. white sugar
1 1/2 tsps. hot sauce
1/2 tsp. ground white pepper
1/2 tsp. freshly ground black pepper
2 (10 oz.) thick bone-in center cut pork chops
1/4 cup red wine vinegar
3 tbsps. white sugar
2 tbsps. hot mustard powder
1 egg yolk
1/3 cup creme fraiche
1 tsp. Dijon mustard
1/4 tsp. ground turmeric
Cayenne pepper to taste

Directions:
1. Combine hoisin sauce, garlic, soy sauce, ginger, 1 tbsp. red wine vinegar, rice vinegar, sherry vinegar, sesame oil, 2 tsps. sugar, hot sauce, white pepper, and black pepper in a large bowl. Whisk thoroughly and set aside.

2. Place pork chops in a resealable freezer bag; pour slightly more than 1/2 the marinade into freezer bag over pork chops. Seal bag and refrigerate for 6 to 8 hours.
3. Reserve remaining marinade.
4. Combine 1/4 cup red wine vinegar, 3 tbsps. sugar, 2 tbsps. hot mustard powder, and egg yolk in a small saucepan over medium-low heat. Whisk until slightly thickened, about 5 minutes; remove from heat.
5. Stir in creme fraiche, Dijon mustard, turmeric, and cayenne pepper. Refrigerate until needed.
6. Remove pork chops from marinade and pat dry using paper towel.
7. Preheat an outdoor grill for high heat, and lightly oil the grate.
8. Cook pork chops on the preheated grill until browned grill marks appear, about 4 minutes per side.
9. Move pork chops from directly above heat source.
10. Continue cooking over indirect medium heat, brushing the remaining marinade on each side, until no longer pink inside, about 25 minutes. An instant-read thermometer inserted into the center should read 145 degrees F (63 degrees C).
11. Serve pork chops topped with mustard sauce.

Grilled Pizza Pork Chops

Ingredients:
5 boneless pork chops
1 pinch salt
Ground black pepper to taste
5 slices tomato
1/4 cup chopped fresh basil
1 tbsp. chopped fresh oregano
2 cloves garlic, minced
2 tbsps. olive oil
5 slices mozzarella cheese

Directions:
1. Preheat an outdoor grill for medium heat.
2. Season the pork chops with salt and black pepper and arrange in the bottom of a disposable aluminum pan; top each with a tomato slice.
3. Divide the basil, oregano, and garlic between the pork chops; drizzle with the olive oil.
4. Cover the pan with aluminum foil.
5. Cook on the preheated grill until the pork is no longer pink in the center, about 25 minutes. An instant-read thermometer inserted into the center should read 145 degrees F (63 degrees C).
6. Remove the pan from the grill; top each pork chop with a slice of mozzarella cheese, replace the aluminum foil over the pan, and wait until the cheese melts, 3 to 5 minutes, before serving.

Chesapeake Bay Pork Chops

Ingredients:

1/2 cup vegetable oil
1/2 cup apple cider vinegar
1 tbsp. seafood seasoning
2 cloves minced garlic
1 tbsp. chopped fresh basil
1 lime, juiced
Cracked black pepper to taste
8 boneless pork chops, 1/2 inch thick

Directions:
1. Whisk together the vegetable oil, apple cider vinegar, seafood seasoning, minced garlic, basil, lime juice, and black pepper in a bowl, and pour into a resealable plastic bag.
2. Add the pork chops, coat with the marinade, squeeze out excess air, and seal the bag. Marinate in the refrigerator for 4 to 6 hours, flipping periodically.
3. Preheat an outdoor grill for medium-high heat, and lightly oil the grate.
4. Remove the pork chops from the bags. Discard excess marinade.
5. Grill until the pork is no longer pink in the center, 5 to 7 minutes per side.
6. An instant-read thermometer inserted into the center should read 145 degrees F (63 degrees C).

Marinated Pineapple Pork Chops

Ingredients:
1 medium onion, finely chopped
1/4 cup Sauterne wine

1/4 cup soy sauce
2 tbsps. vegetable oil
1 tbsp. dry mustard
6 (1/2-inch thick) pork chops
1 (15.25 oz.) can crushed pineapple
3 tbsps. brown sugar

Directions:
1. In a medium container, mix onion, Sauterne wine, soy sauce, vegetable oil, and dry mustard.
2. Place pork chops in the mixture.
3. Cover, and marinate in the refrigerator 8 hours, or overnight.
4. Turn pork chops once while marinating.
5. Prepare an outdoor grill for high heat, and lightly oil grate.
6. Arrange pork chops on the grill, and cook 5 to 7 minutes on each side, to an internal temperature of 145 degrees F (63 degrees C).
7. Top with crushed pineapple and brown sugar before removing from heat. Discard remaining marinade.

Cherry Chutney Grilled Chops

Ingredients:

2 cups cider vinegar
2 tsps. salt
1 tsp. garlic powder
1 tsp. dried basil
1/2 tsp. crushed red pepper flakes
8 bone-in pork chops
1 (12 oz.) package frozen black cherries, thawed
1 cup water
1/2 cup white sugar
2 tbsps. chopped fresh mint

Directions:

1. Whisk together the vinegar, salt, garlic powder, basil, and red pepper flakes in a large glass or ceramic bowl.
2. Add the pork chops and toss to coat.
3. Cover the bowl with plastic wrap; marinate in the refrigerator 6 hours to overnight.
4. Preheat an outdoor grill for medium-high heat; lightly oil the grate.
5. While the grill heats, combine the cherries, water, and sugar in a saucepan over medium-low heat.
6. Cook, stirring occasionally, until the sugar dissolves completely, 5 to 10 minutes.
7. Remove the pork chops from the marinade and shake off excess moisture. Discard the remaining marinade.

8. Cook the pork chops on the preheated grill until no longer pink in the center, 8 to 10 minutes per side. An instant-read thermometer inserted into the center should read 160 degrees F (70 degrees C).
9. Drizzle the chutney over the pork chops; garnish with the mint.

Honey Mustard Grilled Chicken

Ingredients:

1/3 cup Dijon mustard
1/4 cup honey
2 tbsps. mayonnaise
1 tsp. steak sauce
4 skinless, boneless chicken breast halves

Directions:

1. Preheat the grill for medium heat.
2. In a shallow bowl, mix the mustard, honey, mayonnaise, and steak sauce.
3. Set aside a small amount of the honey mustard sauce for basting, and dip the chicken into the remaining sauce to coat.
4. Lightly oil the grill grate.
5. Grill chicken over indirect heat for 18 to 20 minutes, turning occasionally, or until juices run clear.
6. Baste occasionally with the reserved sauce during the last 10 minutes.
7. Watch carefully to prevent burning!

Asian Grilled Chicken

Ingredients:

1/3 cup soy sauce
1/3 cup brown sugar
2 tbsps. lime juice
2 tbsps. orange juice
1 tbsp. Thai-style sweet chili sauce
1 tsp. chile-garlic sauce (such as Sriracha)
3 cloves garlic, minced
1/4 tsp. curry powder
4 skinless, boneless chicken thighs

Directions:

1. Place the soy sauce, brown sugar, lime juice, orange juice, sweet chili sauce, chili-garlic sauce, garlic, and curry powder in a large plastic zipper bag.
2. Seal and knead the bag with your fingers to mix all the ingredients and dissolve the sugar.
3. Place the chicken thighs into the marinade, squeeze out the air from the bag, zip the bag closed, and refrigerate for 4 hours or overnight.
4. Preheat an outdoor grill for medium-low heat; lightly oil the grate.
5. Remove the chicken from the bag, pour the excess marinade into a small saucepan, and bring to a full boil for about 1 minute to sterilize the marinade.
6. Grill the chicken thighs until they are no longer pink in the middle and show grill marks, about 25 minutes, basting them generously with the sterilized marinade as they grill.

Grilled Chicken Adobo

Ingredients:
1 1/2 cups soy sauce
1 1/2 cups water
3/4 cup vinegar
3 tbsps. honey
1 1/2 tbsps. minced garlic
3 bay leaves
1/2 tsp. black pepper
3 pounds skinless, boneless chicken thighs

Directions:
1. Preheat an outdoor grill for high heat, and lightly oil grate.
2. In a large pot, mix soy sauce, water, vinegar, honey, garlic, bay leaves, and pepper.
3. Bring the mixture to a boil, and place the chicken into the pot.
4. Reduce heat, cover, and cook 35 to 40 minutes.
5. Remove chicken, drain on paper towels, and set aside.
6. Discard bay leaves. Return the mixture to a boil, and cook until reduced to about 1 1/2 cups.
7. Place chicken on the prepared grill, about 5 minutes on each side, until browned and crisp.
8. Serve with the remaining soy sauce mixture.

Grilled Chicken Teriyaki

Ingredients:
4 skinless, boneless chicken breast halves
1 cup teriyaki sauce

1/4 cup lemon juice
2 tsps. minced fresh garlic
2 tsps. sesame oil
   Directions:
1. Place chicken, teriyaki sauce, lemon juice, garlic, and sesame oil in a large resealable plastic bag. Seal bag, and shake to coat.
2. Place in refrigerator for 24 hours, turning every so often.
3. Preheat grill for high heat.
4. Lightly oil the grill grate.
5. Remove chicken from bag, discarding any remaining marinade.
6. Grill for 6 to 8 minutes each side, or until juices run clear when chicken is pierced with a fork.

Grilled Lemon Chicken

Ingredients:
- 1/2 cup fresh lemon juice
- 1/2 cup soy sauce
- 1/2 tsp. ground ginger
- 1/4 tsp. ground black pepper
- 4 (6 oz.) skinless, boneless chicken breast halves

Directions:
1. Rinse chicken breasts and pat dry with paper towels.
2. Stir together the lemon juice, soy sauce, ginger, and black pepper in a bowl; pour into a large, resealable plastic bag.
3. Add the chicken breasts, seal the bag, and massage to evenly coat chicken with lemon juice mixture.
4. Place in refrigerator to marinate at least 20 minutes, or up to 24 hours.
5. Preheat an outdoor grill for medium-high heat.
6. Lightly oil grill grate, and place about 4 inches from heat source.
7. Drain and discard marinade from the bag, and place chicken on preheated grill.
8. Cook until chicken is no longer pink and juices run clear, 6 to 8 minutes on each side.

Rosemary Lemon Grilled Chicken

Ingredients:

1/2 cup butter
1/2 cup fresh rosemary
3 cloves garlic
1 lemon, zested
1/4 cup fresh lemon juice
6 (6 oz.) skinless, boneless chicken breast halves
Salt and pepper to taste

Directions:

1. In a food processor, thoroughly blend together the butter, rosemary, garlic, lemon zest, and lemon juice.
2. Pour 1/3 of blended mixture into a small bowl for marinade.
3. Cover remaining mixture, and set aside.
4. Lightly season chicken breasts with salt and pepper. Rub chicken breasts with the marinade mixture.
5. Place chicken breasts on a platter, cover, and refrigerate 3 hours.
6. Preheat an outdoor grill for high heat and lightly oil grate.
7. Pour half of the reserved rosemary and lemon mixture into a bowl for basting.
8. Cover remaining mixture, and set aside for topping cooked chicken.
9. Grill chicken breasts 4 minutes on each side, basting with rosemary and lemon basting mixture.
10. Remove chicken breasts from grill, and top with small scoops of the remaining topping mixture.

Lime-Tarragon Grilled Chicken

Ingredients:

1/2 cup olive oil
1/2 cup fresh lime juice
2 tbsps. chopped onion
2 tsps. dried tarragon
1 tsp. salt
1/2 tsp. hot sauce
Salt and pepper to taste
2 lbs. bone-in chicken thighs

Directions:

1. Place olive oil, lime juice, onion, tarragon, salt, and hot sauce into a large, resealable plastic bag; shake to mix.
2. Add chicken thighs, coat with marinade, squeeze out air, and refrigerate for at least 4 hours.
3. Preheat an outdoor grill for medium heat and lightly oil grate.
4. Remove chicken from marinade, and shake off excess. Discard remaining marinade.
5. Season with salt and pepper.
6. Grill chicken for about 30 minutes, or until no longer pink in the center.
7. Chicken thighs don't dry out easily, so don't be afraid to cook them a bit longer if needed.

Vietnamese Grilled Chicken

Ingredients:

2 tbsps. canola oil
2 tbsps. chopped lemongrass

1 tbsp. lemon juice
2 tsps. soy sauce
2 tsps. light brown sugar
2 tsps. minced garlic
1 tsp. fish sauce
1 1/2 lbs. chicken thighs
Directions:
1. Mix canola oil, lemongrass, lemon juice, soy sauce, brown sugar, garlic, and fish sauce together in a mixing bowl until the sugar is dissolved; add chicken and turn to coat in the marinade.
2. Marinate chicken in the refrigerator for 20 minutes to 1 hour.
3. Preheat grill for medium heat and lightly oil the grate.
4. Remove chicken thighs from the marinade and shake to remove excess marinade.
5. Discard the remaining marinade.
6. Grill chicken until no longer pink in the center and the juices run clear, 3 to 5 minutes per side.
7. An instant-read thermometer inserted into the center should read at least 165 degrees F (74 degrees C).

Cilantro-Lime Grilled Chicken

Ingredients:
4 limes, juiced
1/2 cup chopped fresh cilantro
2 tbsps. garlic salt
2 tbsps. ground black pepper

1 whole whole chicken, cut into 6 pieces
Directions:
1. Whisk lime juice, cilantro, garlic salt, and black pepper together in a large glass or ceramic bowl.
2. Add chicken; toss to evenly coat.
3. Cover the bowl with plastic wrap and marinate in the refrigerator, 30 minutes to overnight.
4. Preheat an outdoor grill for medium-high heat and lightly oil the grate.
5. Remove chicken from marinade and shake off excess.
6. Discard remaining marinade.
7. Cook chicken on the preheated grill, turning occasionally, until no longer pink at the bone and juices run clear, about 30 minutes.
8. An instant-read thermometer inserted near the bone should read 165 degrees F (74 degrees C).

Grilled Five Spice Chicken

Ingredients:
1 (5 lb.) whole chicken, cut in half
1/2 lime, juiced
1 tbsp. fish sauce3 cloves garlic, crushed
1 tbsp. seasoned rice vinegar
1 tbsp. Chinese five-spice powder
2 tsps. hot chile paste
2 tsps. grated fresh ginger
1 tsp. soy sauce
1/3 cup seasoned rice vinegar
1/2 lime, juiced
1 tsp. fish sauce
1 tsp. hot chile paste

Directions:
1. Score the skin side of each piece of chicken 2 to 3 times, about 1/8 inch deep.
2. Whisk together the the juice of 1/2 lime, 1 tbsp. fish sauce, garlic, 1 tbsp. rice vinegar, Chinese five-spice powder, 2 tsps. hot chile paste, ginger, and soy sauce in a bowl.
3. Pour into a resealable plastic bag.
4. Add chicken, coat evenly with the marinade, squeeze out excess air, and seal the bag.
5. Marinate in refrigerator for 6 hours.
6. Preheat an outdoor grill for medium-high heat, and oil the grate.

7. Remove chicken halves from the bag and transfer to a plate or baking sheet lined with paper towels. Pat chicken pieces dry with more paper towels. Reserve marinade mixture in a small bowl.
8. Whisk together the 1/3 cup rice vinegar, juice of 1/2 lime, 1 tsp. fish sauce, and 1 tsp. hot chile paste in a small bowl. Set aside.
9. Grill chicken, skin-side down, on the preheated grill for 2 minutes.
10. Turn each piece, brush with reserved marinade mixture, and move to indirect heat.
11. Grill, brushing with glaze and turning ever 10-15 minutes, until well-browned and meat is no longer pink in the center, about 45 minutes total.
12. An instant-read thermometer inserted into the thickest part of the thigh, near the bone, should read 180 degrees F (82 degrees C).
13. Drizzle vinegar lime juice mixture over the chicken and serve.

Lemon Basil Grilled Chicken

Ingredients:
6 (4 oz.) boneless, skinless chicken breasts
1 tsp. freshly grated lemon peel
1/4 cup fresh lemon juice
2 tsps. minced fresh garlic
1/4 tsp. salt
2 tbsps. oil
1/2 cup loosely packed fresh basil leaves

Directions:
1. Lightly pound chicken to an even 3/4-inch thickness.
2. Pat chicken dry using paper towels and place in a large resealable plastic bag.
3. Combine lemon peel, lemon juice, garlic, salt, oil and basil in a blender or food processor. Pulse for 30 seconds or until well blended.
4. Pour the marinade over the chicken, seal the bag and turn to coat chicken thoroughly.
5. Marinate in the refrigerator for at least 15 minutes to overnight.
6. Preheat grill to medium-high heat or about 400 degrees F.
7. Remove chicken from marinade and discard marinade.
8. Grill for 4 to 6 minutes per side or until cooked through.
9. Transfer to serving plate and garnish with additional basil, if desired.

Grilled Beer Chicken

Ingredients:

1 (3 lb.) chicken, split in half lengthwise
Garlic powder to taste
Ground black pepper to taste
1 pinch seasoned salt
1 (12 fluid oz.) can or bottle beer
1/2 cup butter
2 tbsps. garlic powder
1 tbsp. seasoned pepper

Directions:
1. Preheat grill for high heat.
2. In a microwave-safe bowl, combine the beer, butter, 1 tbsp. garlic powder and seasoned pepper. Heat in the microwave for 2 minutes, or until butter is melted and mixture is hot. Set aside.
3. Season chicken generously with the garlic powder, ground black pepper and seasoned salt to taste.
4. Brush the grilling surface with oil.
5. Place chicken onto the grill bone side down.
6. Close the lid, and cook for about 45 minutes, or until the chicken skin is starting to blister.
7. Turn the chicken over, so it is bone side up.
8. They will be black and charred, but the chicken meat will be fine.
9. Pierce the membrane of the bone with a fork, and ladle some of the beer mixture into the 'cup' formed by the bones.
10. Throw a tsp. or so of garlic powder on the coals, close the lid, and seal the vents.

11. Repeat ladling the beer mixture into the chicken, and throwing garlic powder onto the coals every 5 minutes, until the mixture is gone.
12. The chicken should be tender and juices should run clear.

Margarita Grilled Chicken

Ingredients:

3 pounds boneless, skinless chicken breast halves
2 cups bottled margarita mix

Directions:

1. Pour the margarita mix into a large resealable plastic bag.
2. Add the chicken breasts, and press out as much of the air as possible before sealing. Marinate 4 to 8 hours in the refrigerator.
3. Preheat an outdoor grill for medium-high heat.
4. Lightly oil the grill grate.
5. Remove chicken from marinade, and discard the marinade.
6. Grill chicken 8 minutes per side, or until juices run clear.

Grilled Hoisin Chicken

Ingredients:

1 (7.5 oz.) jar hoisin sauce
4 bone-in chicken breast halves
4 chicken thighs

Directions:

1. Pour hoisin sauce into a resealable plastic bag, and add the chicken breasts and thighs. Squeeze out excess air, and seal the bag. Marinate in the refrigerator for at least 4 hours, or overnight.
2. Prepare the grill for indirect heat, and lightly oil the grate.
3. Remove chicken from marinade. Discard marinade.
4. Grill chicken over indirect heat, skin side down, for 20 minutes.
5. Turn; grill until chicken is no longer pink in the center, and juices run clear, about 10 additional minutes.

Grilled Honey-Lemon Chicken

Ingredients:

1/4 cup canola oil
1 lemon, zested and juiced
1 tbsp. Dijon mustard
1 tbsp. honey
2 cloves garlic, pressed
2 tsps. Worcestershire sauce
2 tsps. dried Italian herb seasoning
1 1/2 tsps. salt
1 tsp. ground black pepper
4 skinless, boneless chicken breast halves

Directions:

1. Mix canola oil, lemon zest, lemon juice, Dijon mustard, honey, garlic, Worcestershire sauce, Italian herb seasoning, salt, and black pepper in a bowl; pour into a resealable plastic bag.
2. Place chicken breasts into the bag, seal, and squeeze bag with your fingers several times to coat chicken with marinade.
3. Place a second resealable bag over the first and seal to prevent leaks. Refrigerate chicken for 2 to 4 hours.
4. Preheat grill for medium heat and lightly oil the grate.
5. Remove chicken breasts from bag; discard used marinade.
6. Cook chicken on the preheated grill until the center is no longer pink and the juices run clear, 7 to 8 minutes per side.

BBQ Chicken

Ingredients:
- 3 tbsps. vegetable oil
- 1 1/2 cups cider vinegar
- 1 tbsp. salt
- 1/4 tsp. ground black pepper
- 2 tsps. poultry seasoning
- 2 lbs. cut up chicken pieces

Directions:
1. In a small skillet combine the oil, vinegar, salt and pepper and put over low heat.
2. Add the poultry seasoning while stirring constantly; when sauce mixes well and starts to bubble, it is done.
3. Place chicken on hot grill and brush with sauce.
4. Grill for 45 to 60 minutes, turning every 5 to 10 minutes, and brush chicken with sauce after each turning.
5. Grill until chicken is done and juices run clear.
6. Be sure to keep an eye on the chicken as it cooks, as it tends to have flair ups due to the oil and chicken drippings.

Cajun Chicken

Ingredients:

2 cups vegetable oil
2 tbsps. Cajun seasoning
2 tbsps. dried Italian-style seasoning
Garlic powder to taste
2 tbsps. lemon pepper
10 skinless, boneless chicken breast halves
1/2 inch thickness

Directions:

1. In a large shallow dish, mix the oil, Cajun seasoning, Italian seasoning, garlic powder, and lemon pepper.
2. Place the chicken in the dish, and turn to coat with the mixture.
3. Cover, and refrigerate for 1/2 hour.
4. Preheat the grill for high heat.
5. Lightly oil the grill grate.
6. Drain chicken, and discard marinade.
7. Place chicken on hot grill and cook for 6 to 8 minutes on each side, or until juices run clear.

Greek Chicken

Ingredients:
1/2 cup olive oil
3 cloves garlic, chopped
1 tbsp. chopped fresh rosemary
1 tbsp. chopped fresh thyme
1 tbsp. chopped fresh oregano
2 lemons, juiced
1 (4 lb.) chicken, cut into pieces

Directions:
1. In a glass dish, mix the olive oil, garlic, rosemary, thyme, oregano, and lemon juice.
2. Place the chicken pieces in the mixture, cover, and marinate in the refrigerator 8 hours or overnight.
3. Preheat grill for high heat.
4. Lightly oil the grill grate.
5. Place chicken on the grill, and discard the marinade.
6. Cook chicken pieces up to 15 minutes per side, until juices run clear. Smaller pieces will not take as long.

Grilled Buffalo Wings

Ingredients:

3 lbs. chicken wings, separated at joints, tips discarded
1 cup Louisiana-style hot sauce
1 (12 fluid oz.) can or bottle cola-flavored carbonated beverage
1/4 tsp. cayenne pepper, or to taste
1/4 tsp. ground black pepper, or to taste
1 tbsp. soy sauce

Directions:

1. Preheat a grill to medium heat.
2. In a large pot, mix together the hot sauce, cola, cayenne pepper, black pepper and soy sauce.
3. Add the wings to the sauce - frozen is okay.
4. Place the pot to one side of the grill, so the sauce comes to a simmer.
5. Use tongs to fish wings out of the sauce, and place them on the grill for 8 to 10 minutes. Then return to the sauce to simmer.
6. Repeat this process for about 50 minutes.
7. The sauce will thicken. When the chicken is tender and pulls easily off of the bone, you have two options.
8. You can dip one last time and serve for sloppy style wings, or serve right off the grill for dryer wings.

Grilled Game Hens

Ingredients:

1 jalapeno pepper, seeded
1 habanero pepper, seeded

4 cloves garlic
2 tbsps. vegetable oil
2 tbsps. sherry vinegar
2 tbsps. mayonnaise
2 tsps. salt
2 Cornish game hens, halved lengthwise
1 pinch salt to taste

Directions:
1. Blend jalapeno pepper, habanero pepper, garlic, vegetable oil, sherry vinegar, mayonnaise, and 2 tsps. salt together in a blender until marinade is smooth.
2. Place halved hens in a large bowl.
3. Pour marinade over the chickens and turn to coat completely.
4. Cover the bowl with plastic wrap and marinate in the refrigerator for 3 hours.
5. Preheat an outdoor grill for medium heat and lightly oil the grate.
6. Remove hens from marinade, shaking off any excess, place hens on a plate, skin-side up. Discard remaining marinade.
7. Season skin-side of hens with salt.
8. Cook hens on the preheated grill, turning occasionally, until skin is crisped, meat is no longer pink at the bone, and juices run clear, about 45 minutes.
9. An instant-read thermometer inserted into the thickest part of the thigh, near the bone should read 165 degrees F (74 degrees C).

Thai Grilled Chicken

Ingredients:

4 skinless, boneless chicken breast halves
1/4 cup soy sauce
2 tsps. minced garlic
1/2 tsp. red pepper flakes
2 tbsps. honey
1 tbsp. fresh lime juice

Directions:

1. Preheat grill for medium heat and lightly oil the grate.
2. Place chicken breasts in a shallow baking dish.
3. Whisk soy sauce, garlic, and red pepper flakes in a bowl; pour over chicken, turning to coat.
4. Allow chicken to marinate for 10 minutes.
5. Whisk honey and lime juice in a bowl; set aside.
6. Place chicken on preheated grill; brush with marinade. Discard remaining marinade.
7. Cover grill and cook for 5 minutes, then brush both sides with honey lime mixture.
8. Flip chicken and continue cooking until no longer pink in the center and the juices run clear, about 5 more minutes.
9. An instant-read thermometer inserted into the center should read at least 165 degrees F (74 degrees C).

Grilled Sesame Steak

Ingredients:

1/2 cup sesame oil
1/3 cup sesame seeds
4 yellow onions, sliced
1/2 cup soy sauce
1/4 cup lemon juice
1 tbsp. sugar
2 cloves garlic, crushed
1/4 tsp. whole black peppercorns
1 (2.5 lb.) London broil steak

Directions:

1. Heat sesame oil in a skillet over medium-high heat.
2. Cook and stir sesame seeds in hot oil until golden brown, about 1 minute. Transfer seeds and oil immediately to a large glass or ceramic baking dish.
3. Stir onions, soy sauce, lemon juice, sugar, garlic, and peppercorns into sesame mixture until marinade is evenly combined.
4. Place steak into marinade, turning to coat all sides.
5. Cover baking dish with plastic wrap and refrigerate, turning steak often, for at least 4 hours or up to overnight.
6. Preheat an outdoor grill for medium-high heat and lightly oil the grate.

7. Cook the steak on the preheated grill until meat starts to firm and turns reddish-pink and juicy in the center, about 10 minutes per side. An instant-read thermometer inserted into the center should read 130 degrees F (54 degrees C) for medium rare. Transfer steak to a plate, cover with aluminum foil, and let rest for about 10 minutes.
8. Slice across the grain.

Grilled Chipotle Skirt Steak

Ingredients:
1 cup Sherry Cooking Wine
1 cup tomato puree or crushed tomatoes
3 canned chipotle chiles in adobo sauce
1/2 small yellow onion
1 tbsp. brown sugar
1 tbsp. vegetable oil or olive oil
2 tsps. ground cumin
1/2 tsp. salt
1 (2 pound) skirt steak or flank steak

Directions:
1. In a blender container, combine sherry cooking wine and remaining ingredients except meat.
2. Cover and run on high until smooth.
3. Trim steak of any visible fat.
4. Place steak in a non-metallic baking dish or sealable plastic bag.
5. Add marinade; turn meat to coat.
6. Cover and refrigerate at least 8 hours or overnight, turning meat one or more times while marinating.
7. Preheat grill to medium-high heat.
8. Drain meat and discard marinade.
9. Grill skirt steak about 6 minutes over direct heat with cover closed. Turn meat; grill with cover closed 2 minutes more or until cooked as desired. Flank steak will take longer to cook.
10. Slice steak into thin strips across the grain. Serve with warm corn tortillas, if desired.

Sirloin Steak with Garlic Butter

Ingredients:

1/2 cup butter
2 tsps. garlic powder
4 cloves garlic, minced
4 lbs. beef top sirloin steaks
Salt and pepper to taste

Directions:

1. Preheat an outdoor grill for high heat.
2. In a small saucepan, melt butter over medium-low heat with garlic powder and minced garlic. Set aside.
3. Sprinkle both sides of each steak with salt and pepper.
4. Grill steaks 4 to 5 minutes per side, or to desired doneness. When done, transfer to warmed plates. Brush tops liberally with garlic butter, and allow to rest for 2 to 3 minutes before serving.

Jalapeno Steak

Ingredients:

4 jalapeno peppers, stemmed
4 cloves garlic, peeled
1 1/2 tsps. cracked black pepper
1 tbsp. coarse salt
1/4 cup lime juice
1 tbsp. dried oregano
1 1/2 lbs. top sirloin steak

Directions:

1. Combine jalapenos, garlic, pepper, salt, lime juice and oregano in a blender. Blend until smooth.
2. Place steak in a shallow pan or large resealable plastic bag.
3. Pour jalapeno marinade over the steak, and turn to coat.
4. Cover pan or seal bag; marinate in the refrigerator 8 hours or overnight.
5. Preheat an outdoor grill for high heat, and lightly oil the grill grate.
6. Drain and discard marinade.
7. Grill steak 5 minutes per side, or to desired doneness.

Barbequed Marinated Flank Steak

Ingredients:

1/4 cup soy sauce3 tbsps. honey
2 tbsps. distilled white vinegar
1/2 tsp. ground ginger
1/2 tsp. garlic powder
1/2 cup vegetable oil
1 1/2 pounds flank steak

Directions:

1. In a blender, combine the soy sauce, honey, vinegar, ginger, garlic powder, and vegetable oil.
2. Lay steak in a shallow glass or ceramic dish. Pierce both sides of the steak with a sharp fork.
3. Pour marinade over steak, then turn and coat the other side.
4. Cover, and refrigerate 8 hours, or overnight.
5. Preheat grill for high heat.
6. Place grate on highest level, and brush lightly with oil.
7. Place steaks on the grill, and discard marinade.
8. Grill steak for 10 minutes, turning once, or to desired doneness.

Beer and Brown Sugar Marinaded Steak

Ingredients:

2 (16 oz.) beef sirloin steaks
1/4 cup dark beer
2 tbsps. teriyaki sauce
2 tbsps. brown sugar
1/2 tsp. seasoned salt
1/2 tsp. black pepper
1/2 tsp. garlic powder

Directions:

1. Preheat grill for high heat.
2. Use a fork to poke holes all over the surface of the steaks, and place steaks in a large baking dish.
3. In a bowl, mix together beer, teriyaki sauce, and brown sugar.
4. Pour sauce over steaks, and let sit about 5 minutes.
5. Sprinkle with 1/2 the seasoned salt, pepper, and garlic powder; set aside for 10 minutes. Turn steaks over, sprinkle with remaining seasoned salt, pepper, and garlic powder, and continue marinating for 10 more minutes.
6. Remove steaks from marinade.
7. Pour marinade into a small saucepan, bring to a boil, and cook for several minutes.
8. Lightly oil the grill grate.
9. Grill steaks for 7 minutes per side, or to desired doneness. During the last few minutes of grilling, baste steaks with boiled marinade to enhance the flavor and ensure juiciness.

Asian Barbequed Steak

Ingredients:
1/4 cup chili sauce
1/4 cup fish sauce
1 1/2 tbsps. dark sesame oil
1 tbsp. grated fresh ginger root
3 cloves garlic, peeled and crushed
2 lbs. flank steak

Directions:
1. In a medium bowl, whisk together chili sauce, fish sauce, sesame oil, ginger, and garlic. Set aside a few tbsps. of the mixture for brushing the steaks during grilling. Score flank steak and place in a shallow dish.
2. Pour remaining marinade over the steak, and turn to coat.
3. Cover, and marinate in the refrigerator at least 3 hours.
4. Preheat an outdoor grill for high heat.
5. Lightly brush the grilling surface with oil.
6. Grill steak 5 minutes per side, or to desired doneness, brushing frequently with the reserved marinade mixture.

Korean Marinated Flank Steak

Ingredients:

4 cloves garlic
1 tsp. minced fresh ginger
1 onion, roughly chopped
2 1/2 cups low sodium soy sauce
1/4 cup toasted sesame oil
3 tbsps. Worcestershire sauce
2 tbsps. unseasoned meat tenderizer
1 cup white sugar
2 pounds beef flank steak

Directions:

1. Place garlic, ginger, and onion in the bowl of a blender.
2. Add soy sauce, sesame oil, Worcestershire sauce, meat tenderizer, and sugar. Puree until smooth.
3. Pour the marinade into a resealable plastic bag or glass bowl. Score the flank steak and place into the marinade. Marinate overnight in the refrigerator.
4. Preheat a grill for medium-high heat.
5. Grill steak on preheated grill to desired doneness, about 7 minutes per side for medium.

Whiskey Marinated Steak

Ingredients:

2/3 cup water
1/2 cup whiskey
1/2 cup pineapple juice
1/2 cup brown sugar
1/2 cup diced onion
1/3 cup teriyaki sauce
1/3 cup soy sauce
1/4 cup liquid smoke
1 tsp. minced garlic
4 (8 oz.) rib-eye steaks

Directions:

1. Whisk together the water, whiskey, pineapple juice, brown sugar, diced onion, teriyaki sauce, soy sauce, liquid smoke, and minced garlic in a bowl.
2. Lie the steaks in the bottom of a baking dish.
3. Pour the marinade over the steaks; refrigerate overnight.
4. Preheat an outdoor grill for high heat, and lightly oil grate.
5. Grill steaks to desired doneness, 3 to 5 minutes per side for medium-rare. Allow steaks to rest for 5 to 10 minutes before serving.

Port Wine Marinaded Flank Steak

Ingredients:
1/2 cup lemon juice
3/4 cup orange juice
1/4 cup honey
3/4 cup olive oil
1 cup port wine
1 (2 inch) piece fresh ginger, grated
5 cloves garlic, sliced
2 1/2 lbs. flank steak

Directions:
1. Whisk together the lemon juice, orange juice, honey, olive oil, port, ginger, and garlic in a large glass or ceramic bowl.
2. Add the flank steak, and toss to evenly coat.
3. Cover the bowl with plastic wrap, and marinate in the refrigerator 1 hour to overnight.
4. Preheat an outdoor grill for medium-high heat, and lightly oil the grate.
5. Cook the steaks until they are browned on the outside and red in the center, about 3 minutes per side. An instant-read thermometer inserted into the center should read 125 degrees F (52 degrees C).
6. Slice the steak thinly across the grain before serving.

Mango Spiced Steak Skewers

Ingredients:
1/4 cup Dijon mustard
1/4 cup honey
1/4 cup mango preserves
1/2 cup apple juice
1/4 cup teriyaki sauce
1 tbsp. honey
1/2 cup mango preserves
1 clove garlic, minced
1 tsp. cayenne pepper
1 tsp. kosher salt
1/2 tsp. ground black pepper
2 tbsps. olive oil
1 lb. flank steak, sliced across the grain 3/8-inch thick
10 bamboo skewers, soaked in water for 20 minutes

Directions:
1. Stir together Dijon mustard, 1/4 cup honey, and 1/4 cup mango preserves in a small bowl to make a dipping sauce; set aside. Whisk together the apple juice, teriyaki sauce, 1 tbsp. honey, 1/2 cup mango preserves, garlic, cayenne pepper, salt, and black pepper in a bowl until blended.
2. Add sliced flank steak and toss to coat. Set aside to marinate 10 minutes.
3. Preheat an outdoor grill for medium-high heat and lightly oil grate.
4. Remove the steak from the marinade, and discard the remaining marinade. Thread the steak strips onto the soaked skewers.

5. Cook on the preheated grill to desired degree of doneness, about 1 minute on each side for medium. Serve accompanied by the Dijon dipping sauce.

Margarita Grilled Shrimp

Ingredients:

1 pound shrimp, peeled and deveined
3 tbsps. olive oil
3 tbsps. chopped fresh cilantro
2 tbsps. fresh lime juice
2 cloves garlic, minced
2 tsps. tequila
1/4 tsp. cayenne pepper
1/4 tsp. salt
4 bamboo skewers, soaked in water for 20 minutes

Directions:

1. Stir shrimp, olive oil, cilantro, lime juice, garlic, tequila, cayenne pepper, and salt together in a bowl.
2. Cover the bowl with plastic wrap and refrigerate shrimp in marinade for 30 minutes.
3. Preheat an outdoor grill for high heat and lightly oil grate.
4. Remove shrimp from bowl and thread onto skewers; discard marinade.
5. Cook on the preheated grill until shrimp turn pink, 2 to 3 minutes per side.

Honey Grilled Shrimp

Ingredients:

1/2 tsp. garlic powder
1/4 tbsp. ground black pepper
1/3 cup Worcestershire sauce
2 tbsps. dry white wine
2 tbsps. Italian-style salad dressing
1 lb. large shrimp, peeled and deveined with tails attached
1/4 cup honey
1/4 cup butter, melted
2 tbsps. Worcestershire sauceskewers

Directions:

1. In a large bowl, mix together garlic powder, black pepper, 1/3 cup Worcestershire sauce, wine, and salad dressing; add shrimp, and toss to coat.
2. Cover, and marinate in the refrigerator for 1 hour.
3. Preheat grill for high heat. Thread shrimp onto skewers, piercing once near the tail and once near the head. Discard marinade.
4. In a small bowl, stir together honey, melted butter, and remaining 2 tbsps. Worcestershire sauce. Set aside for basting.
5. Lightly oil grill grate.
6. Grill shrimp for 2 to 3 minutes per side, or until opaque. Baste occasionally with the honey-butter sauce while grilling.

Spicy Grilled Shrimp

Ingredients:

1 large clove garlic
1 tbsp. coarse salt
1/2 tsp. cayenne pepper
1 tsp. paprika
2 tbsps. olive oil
2 tsps. lemon juice
2 lbs. large shrimp, peeled and deveined
8 wedges lemon, for garnish

Directions:
1. Preheat grill for medium heat.
2. In a small bowl, crush the garlic with the salt.
3. Mix in cayenne pepper and paprika, and then stir in olive oil and lemon juice to form a paste.
4. In a large bowl, toss shrimp with garlic paste until evenly coated.
5. Lightly oil grill grate.
6. Cook shrimp for 2 to 3 minutes per side, or until opaque. Transfer to a serving dish, garnish with lemon wedges, and serve.

Grilled Shrimp Scampi

Ingredients:
- 1/4 cup olive oil
- 1/4 cup lemon juice
- 3 tbsps. chopped fresh parsley
- 1 tbsp. minced garlic
- Ground black pepper to taste
- Crushed red pepper flakes to taste (optional)
- 1 1/2 lbs. medium shrimp, peeled and deveined

Directions:
1. In a large, non-reactive bowl, stir together the olive oil, lemon juice, parsley, garlic, and black pepper.
2. Season with crushed red pepper, if desired.
3. Add shrimp, and toss to coat. Marinate in the refrigerator for 30 minutes.
4. Preheat grill for high heat. Thread shrimp onto skewers, piercing once near the tail and once near the head. Discard any remaining marinade.
5. Lightly oil grill grate.
6. Grill for 2 to 3 minutes per side, or until opaque.

Spicy Coconut and Lime Grilled Shrimp

Ingredients:

2 jalapeno peppers, seeded
1 lime, zested and juiced
2 garlic cloves
1/3 cup chopped fresh cilantro
1/3 cup shredded coconut
1/4 cup olive oil
1/4 cup soy sauce
1 lb. uncooked medium shrimp, peeled and deveined
Skewers

Directions:

1. Combine the jalapeno, lime zest, lime juice, garlic, cilantro, coconut, olive oil, and soy sauce in a food processor; blend until smooth.
2. Place the shrimp in a large bowl.
3. Pour the sauce over the shrimp and toss to coat.
4. Cover and allow to marinate at least 2 hours.
5. Preheat an outdoor grill for medium-high heat and lightly oil the grate.
6. Thread the shrimp onto skewers, piercing each shrimp near the head and tail.
7. Cook the skewers on the preheated grill, turning frequently until nicely browned on all sides and the meat is no longer pink in the center, 2 to 3 minutes per side.

Sweet and Spicy Grilled Shrimp

Ingredients:

6 bamboo skewers, soaked in water for 20 minutes

1/2 cup chile-garlic sauce

1/2 cup honey

1 pound medium shrimp, peeled and deveined

Directions:

1. Preheat grill for medium heat and lightly oil the grate.
2. Stir chile-garlic sauce and honey together in a small bowl.
3. Thread shrimp onto soaked bamboo skewers, piercing through the head and tail ends.
4. Cook the skewers on the preheated grill, frequently turning and basting with the sauce mixture, until shrimp are firm and pink on all sides, about 10 minutes.

Grilled Garlic and Herb Shrimp

Ingredients:
1 1/2 tsps. kosher salt
1/2 tsp. lemon zest
3 cloves garlic, thinly sliced
3 tbsps. chopped fresh basil leaves
3 tbsps. chopped fresh flat-leaf parsley
1 tbsp. chopped fresh oregano leaves
1 tbsp. chopped fresh lemon thyme leaves
4 tbsps. olive oil, divided, or as needed
2 lbs. extra large shrimp (16-20), peeled and deveined, tail left onskewers

Sauce Ingredients:
1 tbsp. olive oil
1/2 lemon, juiced
1/2 tsp. red pepper flakes
1 pinch cayenne pepper
Salt and ground black pepper to taste
1 lemon, cut into wedge

Directions:
1. Place salt, lemon zest, and 3 cloves garlic in bowl of a mortar and pestle. Pound with the pestle until mixture begins to form a paste, about 2 minutes.
2. Add chopped basil, parsley, oregano, and thyme and pound with pestle until mixture begin to come together, about 5 minutes.
3. Drizzle about 1 tbsp. of the olive oil into herb mixture. Grind together until mixture begins to form a sauce for marinating, about 1 minute.
4. Pour in the remaining 3 tbsps. olive oil.

5. Stir mixture with a spoon until mixture is thoroughly combined, adding additional olive oil as needed.
6. Mixture should be fairly thick but pourable.
7. Place shrimp in a large bowl and mix in about 2/3 of the sauce, reserving 1/3 for serving.
8. Stir until shrimp are evenly coated with the sauce, about 2 minutes. Transfer shrimp to a resealable plastic bag. Refrigerate 2 to 3 hours.
9. Cover and refrigerate remaining sauce.
10. Preheat an outdoor grill for high heat and lightly oil the grate.
11. Thread shrimp onto skewers (pierce each twice, once through large part of shrimp, once through small part).
12. Place skewers on hot grill.
13. Cook on each side until shrimp are bright pink and opaque and exterior is beginning to caramelize, 2 to 3 minutes per side. Transfer skewers to serving platter.
14. Pour remaining sauce into mixing bowl. Whisk in 1 tbsp. olive oil, lemon juice, red pepper flakes, cayenne pepper, salt and black pepper. Spoon sauce over shrimp. Serve with lemon wedges.

Basil Shrimp

Ingredients:

2 1/2 tbsps. olive oil
1/4 cup butter, melted
1 1/2 lemons, juiced
3 tbsps. Dijon mustard
1/2 cup minced fresh basil leaves
3 cloves garlic, minced
Salt to taste
White pepper
3 lbs. fresh shrimp, peeled and deveined
Skewers

Directions:

1. In a shallow, non-porous dish or bowl, mix together olive oil and melted butter.
2. Stir in lemon juice, mustard, basil, and garlic, and season with salt and white pepper.
3. Add shrimp, and toss to coat.
4. Cover, and refrigerate for 1 hour.
5. Preheat grill to high heat.
6. Remove shrimp from marinade, and thread onto skewers. Discard marinade.
7. Lightly oil grill grate, and arrange skewers on preheated grill.
8. Cook for 4 minutes, turning once, or until opaque.

Thai Spiced Barbecue Shrimp

Ingredients:

3 tbsps. fresh lemon juice
1 tbsp. soy sauce

1 tbsp. Dijon mustard
2 cloves garlic, minced
1 tbsp. brown sugar
2 tsps. curry paste
1 pound medium shrimp, peeled and deveined

Directions:
1. In a shallow dish or resealable bag, mix together the lemon juice, soy sauce, mustard, garlic, brown sugar and curry paste.
2. Add shrimp, and seal or cover. Marinate in the refrigerator for 1 hour.
3. Preheat a grill for high heat. When the grill is hot, lightly oil the grate. Thread the shrimp onto skewers, or place in a grill basket for easy handling. Transfer the marinade to a saucepan, and boil for a few minutes.
4. Grill shrimp for 3 minutes per side, or until opaque. Baste occasionally with the marinade.

Chipotle Grilled Shrimp

Ingredients:

3 cloves garlic, minced
2 chipotle peppers in adobo sauce, chopped
1 lemon, juiced
1 tbsp. olive oil
1 tbsp. paprika
1 tsp. chopped fresh cilantro (optional)
1 tsp. kosher salt
1/2 tsp. cracked black pepper
1/2 tsp. crushed red pepper flakes
1/4 tsp. cayenne pepper
2 lbs. uncooked medium shrimp, peeled and deveined
Wooden or metal skewers

Directions:

1. Mix together the garlic, chipotle peppers, lemon juice, olive oil, paprika, cilantro, kosher salt, black pepper, red pepper flakes, and cayenne pepper in a bowl.
2. Stir in the shrimp, and mix well to thoroughly coat. Marinate for 30 minutes in refrigerator.
3. Preheat an outdoor grill for medium-high heat, and lightly oil the grate.
4. Remove the shrimp from the marinade, and discard excess marinade. Thread about 5 shrimp per skewer, and grill on the preheated grill until the shrimp turn pink and opaque in the center, about 2 minutes per side.

Spicy Lime Grilled Shrimp

Ingredients:
3 tbsps. Cajun seasoning
1 lime, juiced
1 tbsp. vegetable oil
1 lb. peeled and deveined medium shrimp

Directions:
1. Mix together the Cajun seasoning, lime juice, and vegetable oil in a resealable plastic bag.
2. Add the shrimp, coat with the marinade, squeeze out excess air, and seal the bag. Marinate in the refrigerator for 20 minutes.
3. Preheat an outdoor grill for medium heat, and lightly oil the grate.
4. Remove the shrimp from the marinade, and shake off excess. Discard the remaining marinade.
5. Cook the shrimp on the preheated grill until they are bright pink on the outside and the meat is no longer transparent in the center, about 2 minutes per side.

Cajun Grilled Veggies

Ingredients:
1/4 cup light olive oil
1 tsp. Cajun seasoning
1/2 tsp. salt
1/2 tsp. cayenne pepper
1 tbsp. Worcestershire sauce
2 zucchinis, cut into slices
2 large white onions, sliced into wedges
2 yellow squash, cut into slices

Directions:
1. In a small bowl, mix together light olive oil, Cajun seasoning, salt, cayenne pepper, and Worcestershire sauce.
2. Place zucchinis, white onions, and yellow squash in a bowl, and cover with the olive oil mixture.
3. Cover bowl, and marinate vegetables in the refrigerator at least 30 minutes.
4. Preheat an outdoor grill for high heat and lightly oil grate.
5. Place marinated vegetable pieces on skewers or directly on the grill.
6. Cook 5 minutes, or to desired doneness.

Smoky Grilled Vegetables

Ingredients:
1 eggplant, sliced into rounds
2 red bell peppers, halved and seeded
2 yellow bell peppers, halved and seeded
2 zucchini, sliced
2 large onions, peeled and sliced
4 tbsps. vegetable oil
1 cup teriyaki sauce

Directions:
1. Brush vegetables with oil to coat.
2. Prepare smoker using manufacturer's instructions using either alder or apple chips.
3. Place veggies in single layers on smoker racks. Smoke for about 30 minutes.
4. Preheat grill for high heat.
5. Brush grate with oil.
6. Arrange vegetables on grill, with the peppers away from the center.
7. Cook for 10 to 15 minutes, turning once. Baste with teriyaki sauce frequently. Vegetables will cook at different rates; remove tender pieces from the grill, and continue cooking until all are done.

Herb Grilled Vegetables

Ingredients:
1/2 cup chicken broth
1/2 tsp. dried thyme leaves, crushed
1/8 tsp. ground black pepper
1 large red onion, thickly sliced
1 large red or green pepper, cut into wide strips
1 medium zucchini or yellow squash, thickly sliced
2 cups large mushrooms

Directions:
1. Stir the broth, thyme and black pepper in a small bowl. Brush the vegetables with the broth mixture.
2. Lightly oil the grill rack and heat the grill to medium.
3. Grill the vegetables for 10 minutes or until they're tender-crisp, turning over once during grilling and brushing often with the broth mixture.

Grilled Zucchini Slices

Ingredients:
- 1 tbsp. olive oil
- 1 1/2 tsps. onion powder
- 1 1/2 tsps. seasoned salt
- 1 1/2 tsps. garlic powder
- 2 zucchini, thinly sliced lengthwise and 1/4-inch wide

Directions:
1. Whisk olive oil, onion powder, seasoned salt, and garlic powder together in a bowl; add zucchini and marinate for about 30 minutes.
2. Preheat grill for medium heat and lightly oil the grate.
3. Grill zucchini slices on the preheated grill for about 10 minutes. Flip and grill until edges are crisp and grill marks are present, about 10 minutes more.

Balsamic Grilled Zucchini

Ingredients:

2 zucchinis, quartered lengthwise
2 tsps. olive oil
1/2 tsp. garlic powder
1 tsp. Italian seasoning
1 pinch salt
2 tbsps. balsamic vinegar

Directions:

1. Preheat grill to medium-low heat and lightly oil the grate.
2. Brush zucchini with olive oil.
3. Sprinkle garlic powder, Italian seasoning, and salt over zucchini.
4. Cook on preheated grill until beginning to brown, 3-4 minutes per side. Brush balsamic vinegar over the zucchini and continue cooking 1 minute more. Serve immediately.

Grilled Garlic Parmesan Zucchini

Ingredients:

3 zucchini
3 tbsps. butter, softened
2 cloves garlic, minced
1 tbsp. chopped fresh parsley
1/2 cup freshly grated Parmesan cheese

Directions:

1. Preheat an outdoor grill for medium-high heat, and lightly oil the grate.
2. Cut the zucchini in half crosswise, then slice each half into 3 slices lengthwise, making 6 slices per zucchini.
3. Mix the butter, garlic, and parsley in a bowl, and spread the mixture on both sides of each zucchini slice.
4. Sprinkle one side of each slice with Parmesan cheese, and place the slices, cheese sides up, crosswise on the preheated grill to keep them from falling through.
5. Grill the zucchini until the cheese has melted and the slices are cooked through and show grill marks, about 8 minutes.

Grilled Italian Dressing Asparagus

Ingredients:

1 bunch fresh asparagus, trimmed

1/3 cup Italian-style dressing

3/4 tsp. lemon pepper

Salt and ground black pepper to taste

Directions:

1. Preheat grill for medium heat and lightly oil the grate.
2. Lay asparagus flat in a 9x9-inch pan.
3. Add Italian dressing, lemon pepper, salt, and black pepper; toss to coat. Transfer asparagus using tongs to the grill.
4. Grill asparagus on preheated grill until tender, 3 to 5 minutes per side. Return asparagus to pan and toss with remaining dressing mixture.

Grilled Soy-Sesame Asparagus

Ingredients:

1 tbsp. toasted sesame oil
1 tbsp. soy sauce
3 cloves garlic, minced
1 tsp. brown sugar
1 1/2 lbs. fresh asparagus, trimmed
2 tbsps. toasted sesame seeds

Directions:

1. Preheat grill for high heat.
2. In a bowl, mix sesame oil, soy sauce, garlic, and brown sugar.
3. Place asparagus in the bowl, and toss to coat.
4. Lightly oil a fine-mesh grill grate.
5. Place asparagus on grate, and cook 8 minutes, until tender but firm. Garnish with sesame seeds to serve.

Grilled Eggplant

Ingredients:

1 large eggplant, peeled and cut into 1/2-inch slices
1/4 cup soy sauce
1/4 cup balsamic vinegar
1/4 cup olive oil

Directions:

1. Preheat an outdoor grill for medium-high heat and lightly oil the grate.
2. Mix soy sauce, balsamic vinegar, and olive oil together in a small bowl. Coat eggplant slices in sauce.
3. Place on preheated grill, carefully, as they will flame up.
4. Cook each eggplant slice until deep brown, about 5 minutes per side.

Grilled Cabbage

Ingredients:

1 head cabbage, cored
1 tbsp. butter
Salt and ground black pepper to taste
1 pound bacon

Directions:

1. Preheat an outdoor grill for medium-high heat and lightly oil the grate.
2. Fill the hole created from coring the cabbage with butter, salt, and pepper.
3. Roll bacon slices and stuff into hole in cabbage. Lay any leftover bacon slices over the top of cabbage.
4. Wrap the whole cabbage in aluminum foil.
5. Cook cabbage on preheated grill until tender, 45 to 50 minutes.
6. Remove bacon from cabbage and cook on the grill until crisp, 5 to 7 minutes; crumble and sprinkle over cabbage.

Coconut and Lime Grilled Kale

Ingredients:

2 (13.5 oz.) cans coconut milk

2 limes, juiced

2 tsps. smoked paprika

1 tsp. sea salt

1 tsp. cayenne pepper

1/2 tsp. red pepper flakes, or to taste

2 bunches kale, leaves separated, stems discarded

Directions:

1. Heat coconut milk in a saucepan over low heat until lukewarm, about 5 minutes; pour into a large glass bowl.
2. Stir lime juice, paprika, sea salt, cayenne pepper, and red pepper flakes into milk until marinade is smooth.
3. Place kale into marinade and press down to ensure all leaves are covered.
4. Cover the bowl with plastic wrap and refrigerate for 4 hours.
5. Preheat an outdoor grill for medium-high heat and lightly oil the grate.
6. Remove kale from marinade and shake off excess. Discard remaining marinade.
7. Working in batches, grill kale leaves in a single layer until edges are slightly crispy and centers are soft, 45 to 60 seconds per side.

Grilled Fava Beans

Ingredients:

2 lbs. whole fava beans in the shell
2 tbsps. olive oil, or more as needed
2 lemons, divided
1 tbsp. kosher salt, divided
3 cloves garlic, bruised
1 tsp. red pepper flakes, or more to taste
2 tbsps. sliced fresh mint leaves

Directions:
1. Place whole fava beans in a mixing bowl. Drizzle generously with at least a tbsp. olive oil and the juice of 1 lemon.
2. Sprinkle with half of the kosher salt; add bruised garlic cloves.
3. Toss to coat pods evenly, and occasionally as the grill heats up.
4. Grill beans over high heat, about 5 minutes total per side, turning and moving them until they are charred on the outside and the beans inside are soft. Transfer to a serving platter.
5. Drizzle with the remaining olive oil; sprinkle with the remaining salt.
6. Add red pepper flakes and mint leaves.
7. Toss to coat. To eat, split open the pod and eat the beans inside, or serve them on half the shell.

Grilled Cauliflower

Ingredients:
1 head cauliflower, cut into large florets
3 tbsps. olive oil
1 tsp. coarse sea salt

1 tsp. cracked black pepper

Directions:
1. Preheat grill for medium heat and lightly oil the grate.
2. Place cauliflower in a bowl. Drizzle olive oil over cauliflower and season with salt and pepper; toss to evenly coat.
3. Cook on the preheated grill, turning every 2 minutes, until cauliflower is golden brown, 10 to 15 minutes.

Grilled Potatoes

Ingredients:

2 large russet potatoes, scrubbed

2 tbsps. olive oil

Salt and ground black pepper to taste

Directions:

1. Poke each potato with the tines of a fork.
2. Place the potatoes in a microwave oven, and cook on high power for about 5 minutes. Check about halfway through, and turn potatoes over for even cooking.
3. Slice each potato in half the long way and cook potatoes another 2 minutes on high power.
4. Preheat a grill for medium heat.
5. Brush the potato tops with olive oil, and season with salt and pepper to taste.
6. Cook on prepared grill for 15 to 20 minutes, turning once.

Grilled Caramelized Onions

Ingredients:

1 large Vidalia or sweet onion, peeled and cut into large wedges

2 tbsps. softened butter

1 tsp. beef bouillon granules

garlic salt and pepper to taste

Directions:

1. Preheat an outdoor grill for medium heat.
2. Place the onion wedges on a sheet of heavy duty aluminum foil.
3. ot with butter, then sprinkle with bouillon, garlic salt, and pepper to taste. Fold the aluminum foil into a packet, leaving only a small hole at the top to allow steam to escape.
4. Place packet on preheated grill, and cook until the onions have softened, and cooked to a deep, rich brown, 45 minutes to 1 hour depending on the temperature of the grill.
5. Stir the onions after the first 30 minutes, or as needed to keep from burning.

Grilled Sweet Potatoes with Apples

Ingredients:
2 large sweet potatoes, sliced
1 apple - peeled, cored and thinly sliced
Ground cinnamon to taste
White sugar to taste
1/2 cup butter

Directions:
1. Preheat an outdoor grill.
2. In a bowl, toss the sweet potato and apple slices with the cinnamon and sugar. Divide the mixture into 4 portions, places each on a large piece of aluminum foil. Top each with an equal amount of butter. Tightly seal foil around each portion.
3. Place foil packets on the grill, and cook 40 minutes, turning every 5 to 10 minutes, until potatoes and apples are tender.

Grilled Portobello Mushrooms with Blue Cheese

Ingredients:

4 portobello mushrooms, stems removed

4 oz. crumbled blue cheese

Directions:

1. Preheat an outdoor grill for medium-high heat and lightly oil the grate.
2. Place mushrooms, gill-side up, on a work surface; fill each with 1 oz. blue cheese.
3. Cook mushrooms, blue cheese-side up, on the preheated grill, rotating every 5 minutes, until mushrooms are tender and cheese is melted, about 20 minutes.

Pesto Stuffed Grilled Portobellos

Ingredients:
6 portobello mushrooms
1 tbsp. olive oil
1 small shallot, minced
1 clove garlic, minced
1 splash Chardonnay wine, or as desired
3 tbsps. pesto2 tbsps. pine nuts
1/2 cup shredded Italian 3-cheese blend

Directions:
1. Remove stems from mushrooms and finely chop stems.
2. Heat olive oil in a skillet over medium heat; cook and stir chopped mushroom stems, shallot, and garlic until softened, about 5 minutes.
3. Pour wine into the skillet; cook and stir mixture using a wooden spoon until liquid is evaporated, 1 to 2 minutes. Cool mixture to room temperature, about 10 minutes.
4. Preheat an outdoor grill for medium heat and lightly oil the grate.
5. Brush the olive oil mixture over the top each mushroom and place, top-side up, on a grilling pan.
6. Mix pesto and pine nuts with the mushroom stem mixture together in a bowl; spoon into each mushroom.
7. Sprinkle Italian cheese blend over the filling.
8. Grill mushrooms on the preheated grill until edges are blackened and stuffing is bubbling, about 10 minutes.

# Part 2

Introduction

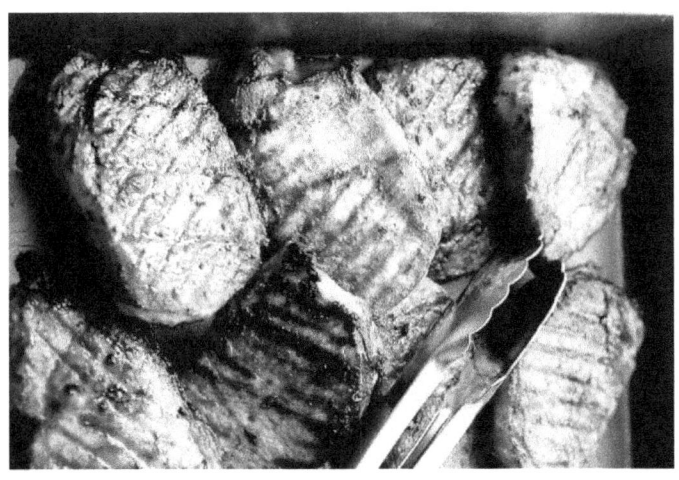

Greetings readers! Thank you so much for purchasing my book! Getting the grill fired up makes any family or social gathering more exciting than a traditional meal around the table. I'm sure you will all agree, there is definitely something fun and magical about cooking around a fire with your loved ones.

Grilling gives the food a delicious smokey flavor, when combined with an array of succulent ingredients, the meal becomes simply irresistible. The great thing about grilling food is that you don't need any culinary skills to get stuck in. Even if you have never touched a grill in your life, as long as you know how to follow instructions, you will easily be able to make any of the recipes in this book.

In case you are wondering about what side dishes to combine with these grilled recipes, here is a list to choose from:

- Broccoli salad
- Sweet potatoes
- Salt and vinegar potatoes
- Brown sugar bacon baked beans
- Corn bread
- Potato salad
- White barbeque sauce
- Chipotle pasta salad
- Roast potatoes
- Coleslaw
- Corn flour biscuits
- Shrimp pasta salad
- Grilled corn salad

This is just a short list, I'm sure you can come up with a lot more ideas now that your taste buds have been stimulated.

Your mouth is probably watering now waiting to get stuck in and make your first recipe so I'm going to stop typing and let you get on with it!

Bon appetite!

1: Grilled Chicken with Pineapple

(Tangy grilled chicken served with sweet pineapple)
(Preparation time: 1 hour 15 minutes/Serves: 6 servings)

Ingredients

- Chicken tenders, 2 pounds
- 1 cup of sweet chili sauce
- ¼ cup of fresh pineapple juice
- ¼ cup of honey

Directions

1. Combine the honey, pineapple juice and sweet chili sauce in a medium bowl. Whisk together thoroughly.
2. Put ¼ cup of the mixture to one side.
3. Coat the chicken in the sauce.
4. Place a lid over the bowl and leave it in the fridge for 30 minutes to marinate.
5. Heat the grill to a high heat.

6. Take the chicken out of the marinade and grill for 5 minutes on each side.
7. Use the reserved sauce to brush over the chicken.
8. Continue to grill for a further 1 minute on each side.
9. Take the chicken off the grill and let it rest for 5 minutes before servings.

2: Stuffed Grilled Bell Peppers

(Delicious bell peppers stuffed with rice, corn, cheddar cheese and salsa)
(Preparation time: 25 minutes/Serves: 5 servings)
Ingredients
- 5 red bell peppers, tops removed and seeded
- 1 cup of uncooked rice
- 1 cup of frozen and thawed corn
- 1 cup of shredded cheddar cheese
- ½ a cup of minced onions
- ½ a cup of mild salsa
- 1 can of chili beans
- 1 teaspoon of ground cumin
- ½ a teaspoon of cayenne pepper

- ½ a teaspoon of salt

Directions

1. Cook the rice according to the instructions on the packet.
2. Slice the red peppers in half.
3. Heat the grill to a medium temperature.
4. Transfer the rice into a large bowl and add half a cup of the shredded cheese, the corn, minced onions, chili beans, a pinch of salt and the cayenne pepper. Stir to combine.
5. Fill the bell peppers with the rice mixture.
6. Place the bell peppers onto the grill and cook for 10 minutes.
7. Wrap the bread up in foil, place it on the grill and cook for 20 minutes. Make sure that you flip the bread over after 10 minutes.
8. Remove from the grill and serve.

4: Philly Grilled Cheesesteak Sandwich

(Tasty grilled cheesesteak sandwich)
(Preparation time: 15 minutes/Serves: 6 servings)

Ingredients

- 1 loaf of French bread
- ¼ cup of garlic butter
- 2 cups of thinly sliced onion and pepper, cooked
- Roast beef, 4 cups
- Thinly sliced provolone cheese, 3 ½ cups

Directions

1. Slice the French bread into 1 ½ inch thin slices.

2. Butter the top of each slice of bread.
3. Spoon the onion and pepper mixture onto each slice of bread.
4. Spoon the beef onto the slices of bread.
5. Place 1 slice of cheese onto each slice of bread.
6. Cover with the remaining bread.
7. Roll out a large sheet of aluminium foil and spray it with cooking spray.
8. Arrange the topped bread onto the foil.
9. Place the foil with the bread onto the grill and grill for 10 minutes.

5: Grilled Jalapeno Poppers Wrapped in Bacon

(Spicy jalapeno peppers wrapped in bacon)
(Preparation time: 20 minutes/Serves: 12 servings)

Ingredients

- 6 whole jalapeño peppers
- Soft cream cheese, 6 ounces
- 1 minced green onion
- ½ a teaspoon of garlic powder
- Sharp cheddar cheese, shredded, 1 ½ ounces
- 12 slices of bacon

Directions

1. Slice the stems off the jalapenos and cut them in half.
2. Scoop out the insides of the jalapenos.
3. In a small bowl combine the cheese, garlic powder, green onion and cream cheese. Stir to combine.
4. Wrap one slice of bacon around each jalapeno and poke with a toothpick to secure.
5. Arrange the jalapenos onto a preheated grill and cook for 6 minutes.
6. Flip the jalapenos over and continue to cook for a further 12 minutes until the cheese has melted and the bacon is cooked through.
7. Remove from the grill and serve.

6: Grilled Dijon and Maple Chicken

(Delightful grilled chicken bathed in Digon mustard and maple)
(Preparation time: 20 minutes/Serves: 6 servings)
Ingredients
- 6 skinless and boneless chicken breasts
- Maple syrup, ¼ cup
- Dijon mustard, ¼ cup
- 2 tablespoons of soy sauce
- 1 tablespoon of fresh, chopped thyme
- 2 cloves of minced garlic

Directions
1. Preheat the grill to a medium temperature.
2. In a small bowl, combine the garlic, thyme, soy sauce, mustard and maple syrup. Whisk together thoroughly.
3. Make a few shallow cuts in the chicken and brush with the sauce.
4. Arrange the chicken onto the grill and cook for 5 minutes on both sides.
5. Brush the chicken with the marinade, flip and continue to grill for a further 7 minutes.
6. Take the chicken off the grill; let it rest for 5 minutes before serving.

7: Grilled Honey Cilantro and Lime Chicken

(Mouthwatering chicken marinated in lime and cilantro)
(Preparation time: 15 minutes/Serves: 6 servings)
Ingredients
- 2 pounds of skinless, boneless chicken breast
- ¼ cup of fresh lime juice
- ½ a cup of honey
- 2 tablespoons of soy sauce
- 1 tablespoon of extra virgin olive oil

- 2 cloves of minced garlic
- ½ a cup of chopped cilantro
- ½ a teaspoon of salt
- ¼ teaspoon of black pepper

Directions

1. Put the chicken inside a large Ziploc bag.
2. In a small bowl, combine the cilantro, garlic, extra virgin olive oil, soy sauce, honey, lime juice and salt and pepper. Whisk together thoroughly.
3. Pour the sauce into the Ziploc bag, close and shake to combine. Place the bag in the fridge for 3 hours to marinate.
4. Preheat the grill to a medium temperature.
5. Take the chicken out of the Ziploc bag and arrange it onto the grill. Cook the chicken for 5 minutes on each side.
6. Take the chicken off the grill and allow it to rest for 5 minutes before serving.

8: Grilled Barbecue Chicken Hawaiian Style

(Wonderful grilled chicken marinated in barbeque sauce and pineapples)
(Preparation time: 25 minutes/Serves: 4 servings)
Ingredients
- 4 skinless, boneless chicken breasts
- Barbeque sauce, 1 cup
- 1 can of thinly sliced pineapples
- 2 teaspoons of soy sauce

- 1 teaspoon of minced garlic
- 1 bell pepper, sliced into small pieces
- 2 thinly sliced zucchinis
- Chopped green onions for garnish

Directions

1. Preheat the grill to a medium temperature.
2. Prepare 4 sheets of aluminium foil.
3. Arrange one piece of chicken in the center of each piece of foil.
4. Top with the zucchini, bell pepper and pineapple.
5. In a medium bowl, combine the garlic, pineapple juice from the can, and the barbecue sauce. Whisk together thoroughly.
6. Pour the sauce over the chicken and wrap them up in the foil.
7. Place the foil packets onto the grill and cook for 15 minutes. Turn the packets over and continue to cook for a further 8 minutes.
8. Remove the chicken from the grill, open up the packets, baste them with the sauce and sprinkle the green onions over the top.

9: Grilled Kansas City Pork Chops

(Fantastic grilled pork chops Kansas City style)
(Preparation time: 2 hours 15 minutes/Serves: 6 servings)

Ingredients
- 6 thin and center cut pork chops
- 6 tablespoons of packed light brown sugar
- 3 tablespoons of smoked paprika
- 2 teaspoons of garlic powder
- 2 teaspoons of powdered chili
- 2 teaspoons of powdered onions
- 1 ½ teaspoons of salt
- 2 teaspoons of black pepper
- Barbeque sauce, 1/3 cup

Directions

1. In a small bowl, combine the powdered onion, powdered chili, powdered garlic, smoked paprika, light brown sugar and salt and pepper. Whisk together thoroughly.
2. Put the pork chops inside a large Ziploc bag and pour the spice mixture on top. Seal the bag and shake it to coat the pork chops. Leave the bag in the fridge for 2 hours to marinate.
3. Heat the grill to a medium temperature.
4. Take the pork chops out of the bag and arrange them on the grill. Cook for 5 minutes on both sides.
5. Brush the barbecue sauce onto the pork chops and take them off the grill.
6. Allow them to rest for 5 minutes and then serve.

10: Grilled Ranch and Bacon Potatoes

(Beautiful grilled potatoes marinated in bacon and ranch)
(Preparation time: 1 hour/Serves: 6 servings)
Ingredients
- Thinly sliced Yukon gold potatoes, 1 ½ pounds.
- Ranch dressing, 1/3 cup
- 4 slices of cooked bacon, crumbled
- ¼ cup of shredded cheddar cheese
- 2 tablespoons of fresh chopped parsley
- ½ a teaspoon of salt
- A dash of black pepper

Directions
1. Preheat the grill to a medium heat.

2. Grease a large piece of aluminium foil with cooking spray.

3. In a large bowl combine the ranch dressing and the potatoes. Stir to combine, then arrange them on the sheet of foil.

4. Top the potatoes with cheese, bacon, parsley and salt and pepper. Form a packet around the potatoes with the foil and place it onto the grill. Allow the potatoes to cook for 15 minutes. Turn them over and let them cook for another 15 minutes.

5. Remove the potatoes from the grill and serve.

11: Grilled Garlic Steak Skewers Asian Style

(Adorable Steak skewers bathed in garlic, ginger and red onions)
Preparation time: 20 minutes/Serves: 6 servings)
Ingredients
- Top sirloin steak, 1 ½ pounds cut into bit sized pieces
- 1 thinly sliced red onion
- 2/3 cup of soy sauce
- 6 cloves of minced garlic
- Sesame oil, ¼ cup
- Vegetable oil ½ a cup
- Sugar, ½ a cup
- 1 tablespoon of grated ginger

- 2 tablespoons of sesame seeds
- Thinly sliced green onions

Directions

1. In a large bowl, combine the sesame oil, vegetable oil, sesame seeds, grated ginger, sugar, minced garlic and soy sauce. Whisk together thoroughly.

2. Put the steak into the mixture and coat by tossing. Put a lid over the bowl and leave it to marinate for 3 hours.

3. Heat the grill to a medium temperature.

4. Soak some wooden skewers and then thread through the steak and red onions.

5. Place the steak skewers onto the grill and cook on both sides for 10 minutes.

6. Take the skewers off the grill and let them rest for 2 minutes before serving.

12: Grilled Sweet Potatoes

Simple grilled sweet potatoes)
(Preparation time: 30 minutes/Serves: 4 servings)
Potato Ingredients
- Sweet potatoes, peeled and chopped into ¼ inch slices, 2 pounds
- 4 tablespoons of extra virgin olive oil
- A pinch of salt

Dressing Ingredients
- ¼ cup of fresh cilantro, chopped
- 1 teaspoon of fresh lime zest
- 2 tablespoons of fresh lemon juice
- Extra virgin olive oil, ¼ cup
- A pinch of salt

Directions
1. Preheat the grill to a high temperature.
2. Place the potatoes in a bowl and pour the olive oil and salt over the top. Toss to coat.
3. To make the dressing, combine the Ingredients into a medium sized bowl and whisk together thoroughly.
4. Arrange the potatoes onto the grill and cook for 6 minutes on each side.
5. Take the potatoes off the grill and place them into the bowl with the dressing. Coat by tossing and serve.

13: Grilled Rum and Coconut Shrimp

(Appetizing grilled shrimp, marinated in shrimp and coconut)
(Preparation time: 1 hour 5 minutes/Serves: 4 servings)
Ingredients
- 1 can of coconut milk
- ½ a cup of packed, light brown sugar
- ¼ cup of spiced rum
- 2 tablespoons of fresh lime juice
- Shrimp, deveined and peeled, 2 pounds

Directions

1. In a large bowl combine the lime juice, spiced rum, light brown sugar and coconut milk. Whisk together thoroughly and put half of the mixture to one side.
2. Add the shrimp to the rest of the mixture and toss to coat.
3. Put a lid over the bowl and place it in the fridge for 1 hour to marinate.
4. Make the glaze by pouring the coconut milk that was set to one side into a small saucepan. Heat the mixture for 10 minutes until it reduces to half and then remove the saucepan from the heat.
5. Take the shrimp out of the fridge and thread it onto skewers.
6. Arrange the shrimp onto the grill and cook on both sides for 2 minutes.
7. Take the shrimp off the grill, brush it with the glaze and serve.

14: Grilled Harissa Moroccan Chicken

(Delectable grilled harissa Moroccan chicken)
(Preparation time: 35 minutes/Serves: 10 servings)
Ingredients
- Chicken drumsticks 4 ½ pounds
- 1 tablespoon of garlic powder
- 1 tablespoon of paprika
- ½ a teaspoon of onion powder
- ½ a teaspoon of ground cumin

- 1 teaspoon of cinnamon
- 1 teaspoon of salt
- ½ a teaspoon of black pepper
- A 10 ounce jar of mild, spicy harissa

Directions

1. Preheat the grill to a high temperature.
2. In a small bowl combine the cinnamon, ground cumin, onion powder, paprika, garlic powder and salt and pepper. Stir to combine.
3. Place the chicken into a large Ziploc bag and add the spices. Close the bag and shake it to coat the chicken.
4. Arrange the chicken on the grill and cook on both sides for 7 minutes.
5. Brush the chicken with the mild spicy harissa and grill for a further 2 minutes on each side.
6. Take the drumsticks off the grill and allow them to rest for 10 minutes before serving.

15: Grilled Shrimp Melody

(Enticing grilled shrimp mixed with potatoes, corn and chicken)
(Preparation time: 20 minutes/Serves: 4 servings)
Ingredients
- 1 pound of red potatoes cut into ¼ inch thick slices
- 2 sliced ears of corn
- 6 tablespoons of melted butter
- 8 ounces of chicken breasts cut into bite sized chunks.

- Shrimp, deveined and peeled, 1 pound.
- 2 tablespoons of fresh lemon juice
- 2 teaspoons of fresh thyme, chopped
- 2 cloves of minced garlic
- 2 teaspoons of seafood seasoning
- 2 tablespoons of fresh parsley, chopped

Directions

1. Preheat the grill to a high temperature.
2. Arrange 8 pieces of aluminium foil.
3. Divide the potatoes, shrimp, chicken and corn onto the sheets of foil.
4. In a small bowl, combine the melted butter, minced garlic, chopped thyme and lemon juice. Whisk together thoroughly.
5. Pour the mixture over the shrimp mix and season with the seafood seasoning.
6. Wrap the foil around the shrimp mix and arrange on the grill, cook for 15 minutes.
7. Remove from the grill, garnish with the parsley and serve.

16: Honey Mustard Grilled Pork

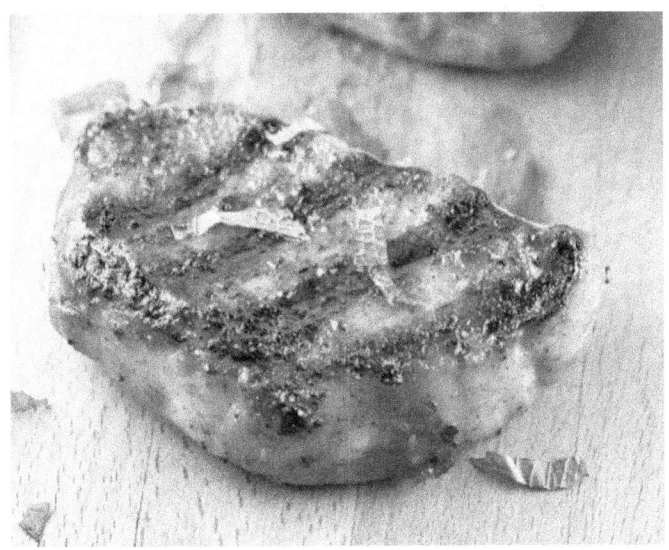

(Simple but delicious honey mustard grilled pork)
(Preparation time: 20 minutes/Serves: 4 servings)
Ingredients
- Four 6 ounce pieces of pork
- Honey, ¼ cup
- 2 tablespoons of Dijon mustard
- 2 tablespoons of grainy mustard
- 2 tablespoons of apple cider vinegar
- 1 tablespoon of soy sauce
- 2 cloves of chopped garlic
- Salt and pepper

Directions

1. Combine all the Ingredients except the pork into a large bowl. Whisk together thoroughly.
2. Add the pork chops and coat. Set the bowl to one side for 30 minutes to marinate.
3. Preheat the grill to high temperature.
4. Arrange the pork on the grill and cook for 5 minutes on each side.
5. Take the pork off the grill, allow it to rest for 5 minutes and then serve.

17: Grilled Chicken with Herbs and Lemon

(Beautiful grilled chicken bathed in lemon and herbs)
(Preparation time: 1 hour 20 minutes/Serves: 4 servings)

Ingredients

- 3 skinless chicken breasts
- Extra virgin olive oil, 1/3 of a cup
- 3 cloves of minced garlic
- ½ a teaspoon of salt
- ¼ teaspoon of black pepper
- 2 tablespoons of fresh chopped parsley
- ½ a teaspoon of fresh, chopped thyme
- ½ a teaspoon of fresh oregano, chopped
- ¼ teaspoon of fresh rosemary, chopped

- 3 tablespoons of fresh lemon juice

Directions

1. Arrange the chicken breasts between two sheets plastic and pound it with a mallet until it is half an inch thick.
2. Place the chicken breasts into a large Ziploc bag.
3. Put the rest of the Ingredients into the bag, seal the bag and shake it to coat. Put the bag in the fridge for an hour to marinate.
4. Preheat the oven to a high temperature.
5. Use oil to grease the grates on the grill.
6. Take the chicken out of the marinade and arrange them on the grill. Cook for 5 minutes on both sides.
7. Take the chicken off the grill and leave it to rest for 5 minutes before serving.

18: Grilled Garlic Bread

(Crunchy grilled garlic bread)
(Preparation time: 25 minutes/Serves: 6 servings)
Ingredients

- 1 loaf of Italian or French white bread
- ½ a cup of soft butter
- 2 tablespoons of garlic powder
- 1 tablespoon of minced garlic
- 1 tablespoon of Italian seasoning

Directions
1. Preheat the grill to a medium temperature.
2. Slice the bread so that they are 1 ½ inches in thickness.
3. Spread the butter onto the slices.
4. Sprinkle the garlic powder onto each slice of bread.

5. Spread the minced garlic over the top.
6. Sprinkle the Italian seasoning over the top.

19: Grilled Chicken Key West Style

(Tasty chicken grilled in true Key West style)
(Preparation time: 50 minutes/Serves: 4 servings)

Ingredients

- 3 tablespoons of soy sauce
- 2 tablespoons of honey
- 1 tablespoon of vegetable oil
- The juice of 1 lime
- 1 teaspoon of minced garlic
- 1 teaspoon of fresh cilantro, chopped
- 2 tablespoons of chopped red bell pepper
- 4 boneless chicken breasts cut into halves

Directions

1. In a small bowl combine the cilantro, bell pepper, garlic, lime juice, vegetable oil, honey and soy sauce.
2. Coat the chicken with the mixture, cover with a lid and allow it to marinate in the fridge for 30 minutes.

3. Preheat the grill to a medium temperature.
4. Arrange the chicken on the grill and cook for 8 minutes on both sides.
5. Remove from the grill and serve.

20: Grilled Asada Carne

(Delicious grilled steak marinated in orange, lime and jalapeno peppers)
(Preparation time: 1 hour and 30 minutes/Serves: 6 servings)

Ingredients

- 2 lbs of skirt steak, fat removed

Marinade Ingredients

- 1 jalapeno pepper, minced and seeded
- 4 cloves of minced garlic
- ½ a cup of fresh cilantro, chopped
- The juice of 1 orange
- The juice of 1 lime

- 2 tablespoons of apple cider vinegar
- Extra virgin olive oil, 1/3 cup
- 1 teaspoon of ground cumin
- 1 teaspoon of salt
- ½ teaspoon of black pepper

Directions

1. Combine all the Ingredients for the marinade into a large baking dish and whisk together thoroughly.
2. Place the steak into the marinade and toss to coat.
3. Place a lid over the baking dish and leave it in the fridge to marinate for 1 hour.
4. Heat the grill to a medium temperature.
5. Arrange the steak on the grill for 7 minutes on both sides.
6. Take the steaks off the grill and let it rest for 5 minutes prior to serving.

21: Grilled Pineapple Sriracha Chicken

(Delicious chicken marinated in Sriracha and pineapple)
(Preparation time: 25 minutes/Serves: 4 servings)
Ingredients

- Barbecue sauce, ¼ cup
- Sriracha sauce, ¼ cup
- Honey, ¼ cup
- Dijon mustard, ¼ cup
- Fresh pineapple juice, ¼ cup
- 4 chicken breasts, skinless and boneless

Directions

1. In a small bowl, combine the pineapple juice, Dijon mustard, honey, Siracha sauce, and barbeque sauce. Whisk to combine.
2. Put the chicken breasts inside a large Ziploc bag; pour the mixture over the chicken. Seal the bag and coat by tossing.
3. Leave the bag in the fridge overnight to marinate.
4. The following day, heat the grill to a high temperature.
5. Take the chicken out of the Ziploc bag and arrange it on the frill. Cook on both sides for 7 minutes each.
6. Take the chicken off the grill and let it rest for 5 minutes before serving.

22: Grilled Brown Sugar Steak in Whisky

(Steak fit for a king – soaked in whisky and brown sugar)
(Preparation time: 1 hour and 20 minutes/Serves: 1 serving)

Ingredients
- Whisky, 1/3 cup
- 2 tablespoons of soy sauce
- 2 tablespoons of packed light brown sugar
- 3 cloves of minced garlic
- 1 tablespoon of Dijon mustard
- 1 teaspoon of red pepper flakes
- New York strip steak, 1 ½ pounds

Directions

1. In a large bowl combine the red pepper flakes, Dijon mustard, garlic, brown sugar, soy sauce and whisky. Whisk to combine and pour the mixture into a large Ziploc bag.
2. Place the steak into the Ziploc bag, seal the bag and toss to coat and leave it in the fridge for one hour to marinate.
3. Heat the grill to a medium temperature.
4. Take the steak out of the marinade and place it onto the grill. Cook for 5 minutes on each side.
5. Take the steak off the grill and allow it to rest for 10 minutes and then serve.

23: Grilled Teriyaki Turkey Burgers with Onions and Pineapples

(Delicious teriyaki turkey burgers with onions and pineapples)
(Preparation time: 35 minutes/Serves: 4 servings)

Teriyaki Sauce Ingredients

- Low sodium soy sauce, 1/3 of a cup
- 3 tablespoons of water
- 3 tablespoons of honey
- 2 tablespoons of rice vinegar
- 1 clove of grated garlic

- ½ a teaspoon of grated ginger
- ½ a teaspoon of sriracha sauce
- 2 teaspoons of cornstarch

Teriyaki Turkey Burger Ingredients

- ½ a pound of ground, lean turkey
- Grated onion, ¼ cup
- 2 tablespoons of teriyaki sauce
- ½ a teaspoon of grated ginger
- Salt and pepper
- 4 buns
- 4 fresh pineapple rings
- 1 thinly sliced red onion

Avocado Spread Ingredients

- 1 ripe avocado
- ¼ cup of non-fat, plain Greek yogurt
- The juice of 1 lime
- 1 teaspoon of honey
- Salt and pepper

Directions

1. In a small saucepan combine all the teriyaki sauce Ingredients apart from the cornstarch and water. Whisk together thoroughly and allow the sauce to boil for two minutes.

2. Prepare the cornstarch according to the instructions on the packet and add to the saucepan. Whisk to combine and continue to boil for a further 1 minute. Take the mixture off the heat and leave it in the fridge until it's time to use it.

3. In a small bowl combine the Ingredients for the avocado sauce, whisk together thoroughly and leave in it in the fridge until it's time to use it.

4. In a large bowl combine the teriyaki sauce, grated ginger, grated onion, ground turkey and salt and pepper. Combine the mixture with your hands, form it into four patties and then set them to one side.

5. Preheat the grill to a medium temperature; use some oil to grease the grates.

6. Brush the pineapple slices and the onion rings with some oil and season with salt and pepper. Arrange them onto the grill and cook on both sides for 3 minutes. When cooked remove them from the grill and place them onto a plate.

7. Arrange the turkey burgers on the grill and cook for 5 minutes on both sides.

8. Toast the buns on the grill for one 1 minute.

9. Arrange the buns on a flat surface, spread a layer of teriyaki sauce onto the buns, add the grilled onions and pineapple onto the buns.

10. Spread the avocado sauce over the other buns, top with the turkey burgers and serve.

24: Grilled Chicken with Lemon

(Simple grilled chicken with lemon)
(Preparation time: 4 hours 30 minutes/Serves: 4 servings)

Ingredients

- 3 pounds of skinless, boneless chicken breasts
- Extra virgin olive oil, 1/3 of a cup
- 2 fresh lemons
- The zest of 2 lemons
- Fresh lemon juice, 1/3 of a cup
- 4 cloves of minced garlic
- ¼ cup of fresh chopped parsley

- Salt and black pepper
- 1 lemon sliced into thin slices

Directions

1. In a large Ziploc bag combine the parsley, garlic, lemon juice, lemon zest, extra virgin olive oil and chicken. Seal the bag and shake to combine. Leave it in the fridge for 4 hours to marinate.
2. Preheat the grill to a medium temperature.
3. Preheat the oven to 350 degrees C.
4. Take the chicken out of the Ziploc bag, arrange it on the grill and cook on both sides for 5 minutes.
5. Heat some oil over medium heat in a large cast iron frying pan.
6. Add the chicken and fry on both sides until it becomes brown in color. This should take approximately 4 minutes.
7. Place the frying pan in the oven for 20 minutes.
8. Take the frying pan out of the oven, let the chicken rest for 5 minutes and then serve.

25: Grilled Soy and Honey Pork Chops

(Heavenly grilled pork chops soaked in honey and soy)
(Preparation time: 1 hour 40 minutes/Serves: 8 servings)

Ingredients

- 8 boneless pork chops
- Salt and pepper
- Organic honey, ¼ cup
- 2 tablespoons of low sodium soy sauce
- 2 tablespoons of vegetable oil
- 1 tablespoon of white vinegar

Directions

1. Season the pork with salt and pepper and place them inside a large Ziploc bag.
2. In a small bowl combine the vinegar, vegetable oil, soy sauce and organic honey. Whisk to combine and pour the mixture into the Ziploc bag. Seal the bag and shake it to coat the pork. Put the bag in the fridge and let the pork marinate for 1 hour.
3. Heat the grill to a medium temperature.
4. Take the pork out of the Ziploc bag, arrange it on the grill and cool for 5 minutes on both sides.
5. Remove the pork from the grill and let it rest for 5 minutes prior to servings.

26: Grilled Crostini with Avocado Caprese

(Delicious grilled crostinis topped with avocado, cherry tomatoes and mozzarella)
(Preparation time: 20 minutes/Serves: 4 servings)
Ingredients
- 8 pieces of sourdough loaf
- Garlic olive oil
- 1 thinly sliced avocado
- 250 grams of cherry tomatoes, sliced in half
- 100 grams of baby mozzarella balls
- ½ a cup of basil leaves

- Balsamic glaze

Directions

1. Preheat the grill to a medium temperature.
2. Arrange the bread on a baking tray and smear each slice with olive oil. Grill the bread until it becomes golden brown and crispy.
3. Top the slices of bread with half of the basil leaves, the slices of avocado, cherry tomatoes, mozzarella and season with salt and pepper. Place the bread back under the grill for a further 5 minutes.
4. Finely chop the rest of the basil leaves and scatter them over the crostini. Sprinkle the balsamic glaze over the top and serve.

27: Grilled Shrimp with Pineapple and Coconut

(Luscious grilled shrimp with pineapple and coconut)
(Preparation time: 1 hour 25 minutes/Serves: 4 servings)

Ingredients

- ½ a cup of light coconut milk
- 4 teaspoons of Original Red Tabasco Sauce
- 2 teaspoons of soy sauce
- ¼ cup of orange juice, freshly squeezed

- The juice of 2 limes
- 40 pieces of large sized shrimp, deveined and peeled
- ¾ pound of pineapple sliced in 1 inch chunks
- Canola oil
- Fresh cilantro, finely chopped

Directions

1. Combine the lime juice, orange juice, soy sauce, Tabasco sauce, soy sauce and coconut milk in a medium bowl. Whisk together thoroughly.
2. Add the shrimp and coat by tossing and leave it to marinate in the fridge for 2 hours.
3. Preheat the grill to a medium temperature, take the shrimp out of the marinate and thread them onto skewers. (If you are using wooden skewers make sure that you soak them in water for 2 hours before placing them on the grill).
4. Brush the grill lightly with canola oil and arrange the shrimp on the grill.
5. Grill for 3 minutes on both sides and then brush them with the marinade.
6. Grill for a further 2 minutes on both sides and brush with the marinade.
7. Take the shrimp off the grill, garnish with the cilantro and serve.

28: Grilled Barbeque Ribs

(Scrumptious grilled barbeque ribs)
(Preparation time: 1 hour 35 minutes/Serves: 4 servings)

Ingredients

- 1 tablespoon of ground cumin
- 1 tablespoon of chili powder
- 1 tablespoon of paprika
- Salt and pepper
- 3 pounds of baby back pork ribs
- 1 cup of barbeque sauce
- Vegetable oil

Directions

1. Preheat the grill to a medium temperature and lightly grease the grates.

2. Combine the paprika, chili powder, cumin and salt and pepper in a small jar. Close the lid and mix by shaking the jar.
3. Cut the membrane sheath from each rack.
4. Season the ribs with the seasoning in the jar.
5. Reduce the grill to a low temperature and grill for an hour.
6. Brush the ribs with the barbeque sauce and continue to grill for a further 5 minutes.
7. Remove from the grill and serve.

29: Grilled Eggplant

(Delightful grilled eggplant)
(Preparation time: 50 minutes/Serves: 8 servings)

Ingredients

- 2 tablespoons of fine sea salt
- 3 medium sized eggplants
- 1/3 cup of olive oil

Directions

1. Dissolve the salt in a large bowl with 1 cup of water. Once the salt has dissolved add another 7 cups of water and then set the bowl to one side.
2. Cut off the stem end from the egg plant. Slice the eggplant into diagonal strips approximately ¾ inches in thickness. Place the eggplant slices into the salt water and soak for an hour.
3. Preheat the grill to a medium temperature.

4. Remove the eggplant from water and pat dry using a paper towel.
5. Arrange the eggplant on a large tray and brush both sides with olive oil and salt.
6. Arrange the slices on the grill and cook on both sides for approximately 5 minutes.
7. Remove from the grill and serve.

30: Grilled Zucchini

(Simple but delicious grilled zucchini)
(Preparation time: 15 minutes/Serves: 8 servings)

Ingredients

- 4 medium sized zucchinis
- 1/3 of a cup of olive oil
- Fine sea salt

Directions

1. Preheat the grill to a medium temperature.
2. Slice the zucchinis lengthwise in half.
3. Arrange them onto a large baking tray and brush both sides with olive oil and sea salt.
4. Arrange the zucchinis on the grill and cook for 5 minutes on both sides.
5. Remove from the grill and serve.

Conclusion

Wow! You made it to the end of the book! I'd like to thank you once again for your purchase because there are so many other books that you could have chosen and so I just want to express my sincere appreciation!

I hope you have discovered some new recipes to woo friends and family at the next barbeque. If you've pre-sampled them, I'm sure you've realized that they will impress the fussiest of eaters!

The next step is for you to truly call these recipes your own and personalize them by adding some of your favorite Ingredients!

I wish you all the best in your grilling endeavors!

www.ingramcontent.com/pod-product-compliance
Lightning Source LLC
Chambersburg PA
CBHW071440070526
44578CB00001B/159